International Series in Operations Research & Management Science

Volume 186

Series Editor

Frederick S. Hillier
Stanford University, Stanford, CA, USA

Special Editorial Consultant

Camille C. Price
Stephen F. Austin State University, Nacogdoches, TX, USA

This book was recommended by Dr. Price

For further volumes:
http://www.springer.com/series/6161

Rahul Saxena · Anand Srinivasan

Business Analytics

A Practitioner's Guide

 Springer

Rahul Saxena
Bangalore
India

Anand Srinivasan
Bangalore
India

ISSN 0884-8289
ISBN 978-1-4614-6079-4   ISBN 978-1-4614-6080-0   (eBook)
DOI 10.1007/978-1-4614-6080-0
Springer New York Heidelberg Dordrecht London

Library of Congress Control Number: 2012952023

Printed on acid-free paper

Springer is part of Springer Science+Business Media (www.springer.com)

For Roshni and Meera, my inspiration and support

For Keerthana who has put up with dad working on this book her entire life

Contents

1 A Framework for Business Analytics 1
A Brief History of Analytics 3
Business: The Decision-Making and Execution Perspective 4
Analytics: The Techniques Perspective 5
IT: The Tools and Systems Perspective 5
A Framework for Business Analytics 6

2 Analytics Domain Context 9
Rational Decisions. 9
Decision Needs and Decision Layers 10
Models: Connecting Decision Needs to Analytics 15
Stakeholders 17
Roles: Connecting Stakeholders to Analytics 17

3 Decision Framing: Defining the Decision Need 19
Big Y, Little Y and Decision Framing 19
Decision Framing for Decision Layers 22
The Airline Partnership Model. 23
Aligning the Layers: Tying the Decision Frame 27
Decision Frames Set Business Expectations 28

4 Decision Modeling. 31
Types of Models 32
Context Diagrams. 33
Data Visualization 34
Mathematical Models. 35
Big Data and Big Models 36
Network Models 37
Capability Models. 43
Control Systems Modeling 47
Expertise. 47
Learning by Asking 49

Learning by Experiment...................................... 51
Value Improvement 53
Optimization Systems Modeling 58
Workflow Modeling... 59
Modeling Processes and Procedures 60
Modeling Assignment and Dispatch 61
Modeling Events and Alerts................................ 62
Transparency, Integrity, Validity and Security...................... 62
Deliverables from Decision Modeling 63

5 **Decision Making** 67
The Role of the Decision Modeler 68
The Decision Making Method................................. 69
Set Context.. 70
Decision Process 71
Step 1: Frame... 72
Step 2: Debate 72
Step 3: Decide 72
Decision Making Roles....................................... 73
Biases, Emotions, and Bounded Rationality...................... 74
Managing Irrationality: Removing Bias from Analytics.............. 76

6 **Decision Execution** 79
Align & Enable 79
Observe & Report 81
Communicate & Converse 82

7 **Business Intelligence**.................................... 85
A Brief History of Data Infrastructure 85
Business Intelligence for Analytics............................. 87
Business Intelligence in the Analytics Framework 88
Data Sourcing 90
Transaction Processing Systems 90
Benchmarks and External Data Sources...................... 90
Survey Tools.. 91
Analytical Output... 92
Data Loading.. 92
Solve Data Quality IT Issues................................... 93
Analytical Datasets and BI Assets.............................. 93
Operational Data Store..................................... 94
Data Warehouse 94
Data Mart 94
Data Structuring and Transformation....................... 95
Business Analytics Input Databases......................... 95
Business Analytics Ready Databases......................... 96
Analytics Tools 96

Reporting 96
Dashboards. 97
Data Visualization 97
Modeling Capabilities 97
Spreadsheets and Microsoft Office Integration 97
Data Stewardship and Meta Data Management. 98
Collaboration 98
Inline Analytics Tools Deployment. 98

8   Data Stewardship: Can We Use the Data? 101
Initial Data Provision. 101
First-Cut Review of the Data 102
Sorts, Scatters and Histograms. 102
Fitness for Use 103
Privacy and Surveillance. 104
Ongoing Data Provision 104
Ongoing Data Sourcing. 104
Ongoing Data Assessment 105
Data Scrubbing and Enrichment 105
Data Scrubbing. 106
Data Enrichment. 106
On Hierarchies, Tagging, and Categorizations. 108
Manage Data Problems 110
Work with IT to Solve IT Issues 110
Work with Business to Solve Business Issues 111
Manage Data Dictionary 111

9   Making Organizations Smarter. 113
Why Bother with Analytics?. 113
Analytics Culture Maturity 114
Actionable Analytics 116
Measure the Value of Analytics 117
Scaling the Decision Culture 118
Lies, Damn Lies and Statistics (or Analytics) 118
Value Management: From Assessment to Realization 118
Make a Plan 119
Criticize the Plan 119
Execute the Plan, Re-assess at Checkpoints 120

10 Building the Analytics Capability 123
Analytics Ecosystem. 123
Placing Analytics Capabilities in the Organization. 125
Analytics Team Skills and Capacity 126
Analytics Scheduling and Workflow. 129
Tracking the Value of Analytics 130
Analytics Maturity Model. 130

11 Analytics Methods... 133
 Process Value Management (Experiment to Evolve) 133
 Capability Value Management 135
 Organizational Value Management 135
 Concept to Value Realization 137
 Criteria for Selecting the Analytics Method 138

12 Analytics Case Studies 141
 Case Study: Product Lifecycle and Replacement 142
  Decision Framing.. 142
  Data Collection... 143
  Data Assessment... 143
  Decision Modeling... 143
  Decision Making 145
  Decision Execution 145
 Case Study: Channel Partner Effectiveness....................... 146
  Decision Framing.. 146
  Data Collection... 146
  Data Assessment... 147
  Decision Modeling... 147
  Decision Making 148
  Decision Execution 148
 Case Study: Next Likely Purchase 148
  Decision Framing.. 148
  Data Collection... 149
  Data Assessment... 149
  Decision Modeling... 150
  Decision Making 151
  Decision Execution 151
 Case Study: Resource Management................................ 152
  Decision Framing.. 153
  Data Collection... 153
  Data Assessment... 154
  Decision Modeling... 155
  Decision Making 155
  Decision Execution 156

References 157

Index... 159

Background and Introduction

This book is aimed at practitioners of Business Analytics: for analysts to perform analytics, managers who lead analytics teams and use analytics, and students who are starting to learn about it. There are several books on the subject, but none that provided a framework with which you can navigate the subject. In this book, you will get an introduction into all the aspects of Business Analytics presented in a framework that we have found to be useful as an organizing principle.

Analytics is a vast new terrain that has emerged from the evolution of fields of study that can be integrated to help conceive of, make, and execute smarter decisions or to go from idea to execution in a more rational way, using data, models, and governance processes that leverage this vast and fast-evolving body of knowledge.

Business Analytics has attracted a lot of press in recent years. The world is moving into a new age of data analysis, and businesses are hopping on to the bandwagon. Partnerships between mathematicians, statisticians, and computer scientists are surfacing into whole new domains of business and imposing the efficiencies of math. This has been the topic of several books and has even made Hollywood sit up and take notice! It is indeed an indication of the times when a main stream movie uses this as the core of its plot line—*Moneyball* is really a case of art imitating life.

The surprising fact in this transformation is only that we are surprised by it. This has happened before, repeatedly! In the past decades, math and computer modeling transformed science, engineering, and medicine. They teamed up again to revolutionize the world of finance. Now the analytics movement has turned its attention to other areas of business. Today, analysts pluck valuable nuggets of information from vast consumer and business databases. Mathematicians are helping to chart advertising campaigns, and they are enabling marketing departments to establish one-on-one relationships with customers. Companies that range from fledgling start-ups (one of the authors runs one) to large behemoths such as IBM are hitching mathematics to business in ways that would have seemed fanciful even a few years ago.

There are companies that have learned to embrace the new world of business and are redefining the way they operate. Mathematical models predict what music we will buy, some determine what type of spaghetti sauce we will enjoy, while others figure out which worker is best equipped for a particular job. The projected growth and development of these models promise to make these current models look like mere stick figures compared to what is in store for the future!

This veritable deluge of data has created a corresponding demand for mathematical skills to analyze it and the IT skills to store and manage the data effectively. New job titles have been created that reflect the changing focus of business. Titles like "Data Steward", "Data Architect", "Chief Scientist", "Chief Analytics Officer", and "Lead - Customer Insights" are examples of job titles that have gone from non-existent to coveted, in a matter of a few years.

The base of practitioners of the field of analytics is growing at an exponential rate. While various books and publications exist for various micro-fields within the realm of analytics, a young professional entering this promising new field is generally overwhelmed by the extent and richness of the material that encompasses his/her chosen profession.

This book attempts to provide the practitioner in the field of Business Analytics a quick overview of the various facets of business analytics. The field has not been around long enough to generate "canned expertise" in focus areas. Most analytics teams are actually cobbled together by drawing upon the mathematically inclined individuals from various traditional business functions. This book touches upon various components that make up the field, and the reader may find pieces more relevant than the others based on his/her background and focus area. Extensive references and links to supplemental material have been provided for the benefit of readers who wish to deepen their expertise in any specific focus area.

Chapter 1
A Framework for Business Analytics

When you think about "analytics", what comes to mind? Is it some kind of specialized work done by data-crunchers? Math and statistics spun by wonks? Something that DVD rental shops use to recommend the next DVD or that casinos use to squeeze more money out of gamblers? Not applicable to you?

In our view, analytics is the rational way to get from ideas to execution. It is only in recent times that analytics as a business function has been attracting attention and organizations are looking for the secret sauce that will enable them to "Compete and Win" using analytics.

Taking a step back from the definition of analytics as a Business Function, let us try to understand how the process of rational decision making has evolved (Fig. 1.1).

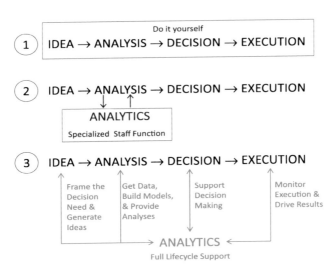

Fig. 1.1 Analytics pathways

R. Saxena and A. Srinivasan, *Business Analytics*, International Series in Operations Research & Management Science 186, DOI: 10.1007/978-1-4614-6080-0_1,
© Springer Science+Business Media New York 2013

Do it yourself: This approach empowers people to use analytics in every part of the cycle from idea to execution. This requires people to think rationally and use data as a "matter of course" during the regular job—i.e., analytical thinking is analytics in action. To make this approach work well, we'll need everyone in the cycle to apply the right analytics techniques and have the time and tools to conduct the analyses. This can be expected to work if people know all there is to know about their own decision domain & analytics, and have the time to conduct the required analyses. As our knowledge has expanded in every sphere and as productivity demands have increased, this is practically impossible. This approach is still applicable in small, specialized teams focused on a limited set of outcomes.

Analytics as a specialized staff function: This is the default operating model of most organizations looking to leverage analytics at present. The analytics team acts as an extension of the traditional staff functions such as Finance, Operations, Marketing, etc. This approach is based on the generally accepted premise of economies of scale and people set up large teams of specialized "analysts" who provide business functions with analytics. This model delivers on its initial promise of economies of scale, but is lacking when measured against the yardstick of using analytics as a game changer.

Analytics providing full lifecycle support: From idea to execution. This is our preferred and recommended approach. It re-connects analytics to the full spectrum of business needs and is implementable because it concentrates analytics talent and tools into a specialized function thereby leveraging the best of both the approaches presented above.

There have been massive improvements in analytics that create the need for specialized analytics professionals and enable their work to be scaled across the full spectrum of business needs.

- Continuous research in statistics and operations research has created a huge knowledge-base with a variety of techniques to address business needs and the talent needed to drive further expansion of our knowledge.
- Sustained improvements in computational power enables us to use analytics techniques that would have taken too long to run using generations of computers.
- Huge volumes of data are generated using computers, and this data can be made easily accessible.
- As people see the benefits of analytics, they demand more, leading to exponentially increasing demand for analytics to be applied in every sphere of endeavor.

These trends favor the dominance of our approach to analytics. These same trends also tee up a fair bit of confusion in people about "what can analytics do for me?" or "what is all this stuff called analytics?" That is because the answer is that it depends upon where your organization is in its use of analytics and where it aims to get.

The ultimate state of analytics can be framed quite attractively: it occurs when the organization uses all available data and the best techniques to generate, evaluate, and select ideas and then execute flawlessly to generate multifaceted value. So when are we going to get there?… And more importantly, *how* are we going to get there?

It depends on where you're starting from, of course. Think about how an organization can measure how good it is in its use of analytics. You will think of various categories: are the best analytics techniques being used by the analysts (Analytics)? Do the analyses get used in the idea to execution cycle by the business-people whom the analysts support (Business)? Do the analysts get the best support and tools from the Information Technology (IT) department?

Successful use of Business Analytics requires collaboration between three functions within a business

- The Business unit that is the consumer of the services delivered by analytics. The Business unit is accountable for its performance, and can use analytics across the analytics lifecycle from idea (or problem) to analysis, decision, and execution.
- The analytics team that helps with the analytics lifecycle by helping to generate ideas, developing analyses, enabling rational decision making, monitoring execution and guiding the steering actions.
- IT that provides the necessary data infrastructure, supports the necessary analyst toolkit, and delivers ongoing model outputs (dashboards, reports, and other such online analytics tools) to the business unit.

This presents a relatively new challenge to all concerned, since never in the history of business has the necessity for the close co-ordination of these diverse groups to work in tandem been more acutely felt.

A Brief History of Analytics

Business analytics has a long history—we can argue that it is at the root of the subject of management itself, since Frederick Taylor[1] used analytics methods from observation to execution. Consultants started to provide analytics services to organizations and would directly work with their business clients. Business analysts started to get employed to assist managers and to take on some analytics roles, especially to make reports. The tools and techniques of industrial engineering and quality control, statistics and operations research, were developed and used by a diverse set of practitioners who provided advice to organizations. Business analytics practitioners treat this as their professional lineage.

IT teams saw opportunities to provide reports for managers, and the concept of Management Information Systems (MIS) was born. These systems were used

---

[1] http://en.wikipedia.org/wiki/Frederick_Taylor

to make reports. This put IT teams in the business of providing analytics to the organization in the form of reports and dashboards, and to aspire to provide "the right information at the right time to the right people". Business Intelligence (BI) and Data Warehousing (DW) teams in IT departments draw upon this heritage.

The functions of planning, decision making, providing direction, motivating, monitoring and control are part of a managers' job. Business schools teach courses in statistics, operations research, etc. to prepare managers for data-driven analytics. As management roles evolved and specialized, managers have increasingly come to rely upon specialized analytics practitioners to work with them. Cycles of restructurings have now created teams of analytics professionals that provide analytics to their parent group. In doing so, the organizations gained efficiency from pooling resources but lost the effectiveness that comes from managers and analytics practitioners working closely and collaboratively.

In order to lay out a framework for successful implementation of Business Analytics, it is critical for us to understand the different approaches of the three functions towards analytics, how "success" is measured in the individual silos, and why they find it hard to work together.

Business: The Decision-Making and Execution Perspective

Business users often see themselves as "consumers" of analytics and expect analysts to build models that can aid in "Grow the Business" or "Run the Business". The decision making process is hardly (if ever) communicated to the analysts effectively. It is generally perceived to be the role of the analyst to "Understand the Business" in order to build effective models. With little or no input going into the model (from the Business), there is a growing sense of frustration with the ability of "Analytics" to help in their work, culminating in a sense of skepticism at the ability of analytics to deliver the promised value.

This distance between Business and analytics teams degenerates into a state of equilibrium where the only analytics demanded are basic reports and dashboards with a sense that "Analytics cannot replace the experience of the business users". In this situation, when they are presented with legitimate cases where analytics have been leveraged successfully the business teams often react with: "But our business is very different and this case is really not applicable here".

The same dynamic applies to how business users work with their IT counterparts, where they are often treated as suppliers of systems and measured by delivering reliable systems that work as specified … without thinking about the fact that for analytics systems the specs must constantly evolve as the business changes every day (or should change) as customers, competitors, employees, suppliers, and markets change.

Business people in the organization need to learn to collaborate with their analytics practitioners and IT teams.

Analytics: The Techniques Perspective

Analysts often see themselves as "Data and Math Experts" and are driven by the sophistication of the techniques and models they build. Since the decision making process that the model is intended to support is not fully understood, interactions quickly degenerate into a "Nice, but how is this useful" mode when presented to the business consumers. An additional challenge constantly referred to by analysts is the lack of data (quality and quantity) to be able to build "State of the Art" analytics models that will take the business to the Promised Land.

It is common to find analytics teams that use IT teams as suppliers of analytics infrastructure. It is rare to find cases where analytics and IT teams collaborate to address business concerns. As a result of this disconnect, when business users need IT to support and scale analytics they deal with the IT teams directly, and cut out the analytics teams. What could be productive three-way collaboration degenerates into hand-offs.

Analysts need to develop methods to collaborate effectively with their business counterparts and IT teams.

IT: The Tools and Systems Perspective

IT generally sees itself as a provider of Business Intelligence (BI) and Data Warehousing (DW) infrastructure and tools to support analysts and business users. In response to the need to develop analytics capabilities in an organization, IT will often launch a project to build or re-build a huge data warehouse to act as a repository of data and enable multiple tools that will enable reporting, dashboards and "analytics" (generally statistical tools). The role of IT ends with making the data warehouse available and operational with the necessary tools as determined by the IT interpretation of business needs. When business managers and analysts are presented a "fait accompli" (a data warehouse, dashboards, canned reports, etc.) they often do not use the expensively-created facilities. In this way, the BI & DW investments become failures by disuse.

> *"Nobody argues with the need for more Business Intelligence; BI is one of the few remaining IT initiatives that can make companies more competitive. But, only the largest companies can live with the costs or the high failure rates. BI is a luxury."*
> Roman Stanek, Founder/CEO GoodData

IT needs to expand their focus to collaborate effectively with their business and analytics counterparts.

A Framework for Business Analytics

While the shortcomings of the silo approach to Business Analytics are fairly evident, organizations lack an understanding of the components that will make it successful.

We propose an "Analytics Domain" where we define how analytics, Business and IT collaborate to drive the "Target Domain"—the real world consisting of the organization and its environment, which reacts to ideas and generates outcomes. In the Analytics Domain we structure six functions: three that form the traditional arms of analytics and three interface areas between these that have hitherto been neglected. These components already exist in various forms within current organizations as they are required functions, but they often struggle in the grey areas between organizations. The relative strengths of the presence of these components determine the degree of success realized by the organization in the quest for excellence in analytics (Fig. 1.2).

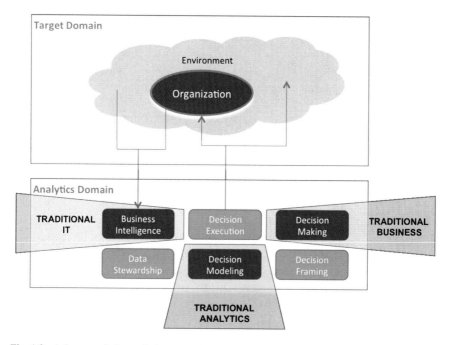

Fig. 1.2 A framework for analytics

Business Intelligence (traditional IT function): to provide the data for decision-making and to provide reliable analytics tools

Data Stewardship (interface function): to measure the quality of data and assess its fitness for use in the decision models

Decision Framing (interface function): to articulate the decision need

Decision Modeling (traditional analytics function): to build and test a decision model that provides rational advice to satisfy the decision need

Decision Making (traditional Business function): to use the decision model to make decisions

Decision Execution (interface function): to convert the decisions into actions in the Target Domain and monitor the results. Flag and control deviations, track actuals versus targets, and drive to results.

We are not inventing new functions, but by calling these out we hope to give them their due importance. We need Business, analytics, and IT to work together in the idea to execution cycle. We often find that all three groups do not fully grasp the magnitude of the task at hand. IT typically asserts its dominion over the data, often by restricting access to it. Analytics teams assert their expertise in making models. Business teams engage selectively and separately with both as "providers of analytics" of different types (Fig. 1.3).

Seen in this context, the proposed analytical framework is simply a natural evolution of disjointed, disparate specialty functions into a collaborative scenario where these functions work together to achieve the goal of analytics (and IT) of providing full cycle analytics support for business functions. The end state of this evolution is a fully developed analytical framework that resembles the diagram below, and we will delve into each of the components of the framework in detail in the chapters that follow.

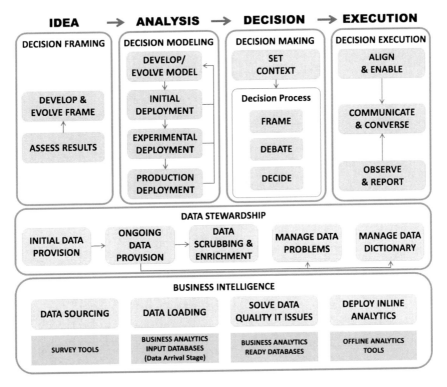

Fig. 1.3 Analytics framework end state

Chapter 2
Analytics Domain Context

The Analytics Domain defined in the previous chapter introduces functions which, while not entirely new, are debuting in the context of Business analytics. Each of these functions is discussed in detail in subsequent chapters, but before one understands what is "in the box" of each of these functions, it is essential to understand the interplay of forces in the Analytics Domain that enables success in the domain.

Much like a shopping list of raw materials does not make a gourmet meal, a strategy of building capabilities in the six functions of the Analytics Domain without understanding the driving factors behind them will not work.

The unifying notion base of the Analytics Domain is that Decision Makers use analytics to make Rational Decisions in response to various Decision Needs.

Let us dwell on that for a minute ... business entities (through their agents, the Decision Makers) are constantly faced with situations that require them to make decisions. These situations occur at various levels of operations and are defined as Decision Needs. Analytics help business entities make data driven (rational) decisions in response to every decision need that may arise.

Rational Decisions

The fundamental objective of analytics is to help people to make and execute rational decisions, defined as being Data Driven, Transparent, Verifiable and Robust.

- **Data Driven**: based on facts that can be verified and assumptions that can be criticized.
- **Transparent**: uses decision-making criteria that are clearly defined (such as costs, benefits, risks, etc.).
- **Verifiable**: resulting from a decision-making model that connects the proposed options to the decision criteria, and a method that assists in choosing the right

R. Saxena and A. Srinivasan, *Business Analytics*, International Series in Operations
Research & Management Science 186, DOI: 10.1007/978-1-4614-6080-0_2,
© Springer Science+Business Media New York 2013

option. The choice can be verified, based on the data, to be as good as or better than other alternatives brought up in the model.

- **Robust**: tested to remove biases that creep in, such as not considering all the criteria or options, calculation errors, presentation biases, etc. This also requires a feedback loop—to watch for the results and help change the selected course as well as the decision-making process.

The benefits of rational decision making are

- Better decisions and focused actions that get desired results.
- Faster and cheaper decision making processes by taking a scientific approach to decision-making.
- Continuous learning and adapting the decision making processes to make decisions better, faster, and cheaper. The process becomes closed-loop and self-correcting.
- Empowerment: with scalable closed-loop and self-correcting (learning) decision making processes, more people can be empowered to make decisions.
- Organizational intelligence: as people learn to take rational decisions, they are said to act more intelligently, and the organization as a whole can be seen to act more intelligently to set and pursue its objectives. The organization can be said to be informed, controlled, responsive, and adaptive.

Decision Needs and Decision Layers

Business entities are called upon to make decisions at various levels that have varying impact periods, scale and scope. People easily recognize Strategic and Tactical decisions (otherwise referred to as Long-Term and Short-Term decisions). We find that it is useful to classify decision needs into four "Layers" based primarily on the scale in which the decision is executed and the degrees of freedom that the decision maker has at his/her disposal (Fig. 2.1).

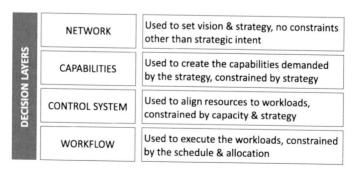

Fig. 2.1 Decision layers

Workflow Layer—These are the decisions that need to be taken as you work. The human decision is generally guided by rules and backed by expertise acquired through training and experience. Systems-driven decisions, such as pricing or discounting, can be of any complexity. Execution-layer decisions occur very frequently and are easily handled by systems that use a set of rules to make the decision.

Real-time analytics are commonplace—they are used whenever we must respond on an immediate basis, for instance to dispatch a police cruiser, to manage concrete-mix trucks, to control a refinery, or to fight a battle. Factory floors have a long history of real time control systems called Supervisory Control and Data Acquisition (SCADA), some of them integrated with Manufacturing Execution Systems (MES) that provide near-real-time visibility into the factory and the tools needed to control the machinery. IT Network Management systems such as HP *OpenView* or CA *Unicenter* track the state of a network and provide tools to manage it. More recently the IT departments have started to mine log files soon after an event is logged so that they can provide visibility to a different data-set, and companies such as Splunk provide commercial tools to do this. Call centers deploy voice analysis software that can run while the customer is on the line to help the call center agent make better decisions, call centers also use tools that can generate offers and pricing "on demand" (i.e., we can run a pricing or discounting algorithm while the customer is on the call).

- **Process decisions** are confined to what the assigned person can do with the work at hand, in the context of a process or procedure that constrains the possible paths and outcomes. The analyses required to support process execution decisions are embedded as rules for people to follow (put into training and procedure-manuals), and as code in automated systems. For example in an airline ticket-booking process, a person works with a system to make the booking. A multi-carrier system such as Travelocity.com will get the options, other underlying systems will determine routes and prices, and the person booking the ticket selects from the carriers, prices, routes, and seats available. In a customer service process, a call center agent can assess the customer's concerns and address them in several ways, including the option to offer discounts, coupons, or escalate (transfer) a customer request to a higher level instead of addressing it at the current level, etc.
- **Assignment and dispatch decisions** occur when the next step in the process can be assigned (or dispatched) to someone else or to a different branch of the process. This provides a way to decide who will do what—as a way to manage inspection, specialization, or overloads (by switching work out of a work-center that is swamped).
- **Alerting decisions** are needed to identify events and to trigger alerts, such as when a project incurs an unexpected cost increase, a shipment is delayed, an important customer lodges a serious complaint, or a key employee takes ill. People need to know what to look for and whom to notify. e.g., we can set an alert to watch for excessively long queues in the checkout lines of a grocery store and a controller (human or machine) can make a decision to open another counter.

Control Systems Layer—In this layer resources are allocated to workloads in order to get results such as revenue maximization, delivery to meet or beat the committed deadline, etc. Control decisions assign resources to workloads while constrained by the capacity and availability of the resources, such as: which person should work on which project, which orders are released for production by which work-center, etc. Analyses required to support control occur once and are re-used many times, often in a highly-automated system that guides the decision-makers. This requires the use of an analytical model that aligns strategy, planning, control and execution, and the quality of the model can be verified every time a work-assignment is done—whether well or poorly. This layer is also, at times referred to as the **Schedule** Layer, since a lot of decisions that happen here have to do with a broad Scheduling problem as seen in traditional manufacturing and operations research.

Capability Layer—These decisions are used to change capacity and set targets, and are constrained by the organization's strategy. At this layer, we deal with making plans, assessing the plan to the reality as the data becomes available (e.g., tracking order-bookings against the quarterly plan), and evolving the plan as needed. These decisions are taken by experienced planners supported by a few repeatable and process-driven analyses that may be automated (such as an order book view that includes plan, committed, and forecasted orders) as well as with ad-hoc analyses conducted on request. Planning analyses are often entirely done using tools such as Microsoft Excel; though systems do exist that successfully grapple with the problems of automating these fast-evolving and people-dependent workloads (e.g., Hyperion Planning or Adaptive Planning for budgeting and forecasting). Planning decisions are taken in conjunction with assessments to address needs such as to increase the team capacity (size) when you plan for or encounter an ongoing increase in demand or to drive the actions needed to realize value from a new system by de-commissioning the old system.

Network Layer—Also referred to as a Strategy Layer. There are few constraints at this layer other than those an organization imposes on itself, such as deciding to focus on margins as opposed to revenues or to reduce environmental impact. These decisions are taken with long time-frames and large impacts and require in-depth analyses that are generally ad hoc and conducted on request.

Of these, we give special prominence to the Control Systems Layer as the primary target for analytics modeling. That is because this layer requires models that include knowledge of the other layers in order to function: effective scheduling requires us to implement the network (strategy), capabilities (capacities and plans), and workflow (execution) models. Network and capability layer models need to get feedback from lower layers, but do not need to model the scheduling and processes. Workflow models, on the other hand, are constrained by higher layers but the demands of rapid execution generally preclude the use of complex models and simulations in this layer. So we can use Control Systems models as the central model that feeds all other models.

By their very nature and time horizon, Network and Capabilities decisions involve parameters for which data may not be readily available. These decisions often involve making several gross assumptions that can never be guaranteed to be of high enough fidelity to support "data driven" decision making in the true sense of the word. Here the use of "model driven" analytics is commonplace—models are used to rationally explore the decision space, and we leverage minimal data or assumptions to help with the exploration and decision-making.

On the flip side, Workflow decisions tend to be so constrained that the spectrum of options to choose from is very narrow. In such a scenario, the deviation of effects between good and bad decisions is minimal and hence leaves little room for analytics to make a "big impact". Though there is a lot of interest in leveraging real-time situational visibility leading to improved business outcomes, a lot of the benefits come from simple decision models that can be run in near-real-time. As control systems models evolve and become faster to run, some of them become available to guide Workflow decisions ... but even so the modeling complexity and speed has to be tackled in the Control Systems layer.

> *The concept of decision layers can be a little confusing to begin with, but one needs to understand that which layer a decision belongs in is driven by the situation that calls for that decision (the Decision Need) more than the decision itself.*
>
> *A common theme in recent years is the outsourcing of "non-critical" business processes to vendors who specialize in exactly those skills and processes.*
>
> *An organization could choose to outsource IT to a specialist vendor and choose to focus its energies on core competencies of the business. This is a strategic decision that is taken at the **Network** layer, and such decisions are binding over multiple years of time horizon.*
>
> *In some cases, an organization could enter into partial outsourcing agreements with vendors to provide contract staff as needed. This allows the organization to acquire a "variable capacity" capability since these contract vendors can be brought on or off very easily. This is a decision at the **Capability** layer.*
>
> *When an organization is faced with a very short term resource crunch, or is in need of highly specialized skills for a short order of time, consultants are engaged to provide specific services. This is a decision to outsource work that is taken at the **Control System** layer. These decisions are usually the result of being unable to "schedule" the right resource internally to complete the task.*
>
> *In other cases, an organization could chose to outsource work on a "task-by-task" basis to partners who have been identified through a decision in the capacity layer. While the capacity is available, it is called upon as needed though a decision in the **Workflow** layer.*

As the example above illustrates, a decision can exist in various layers based on the primary objective or **need** that prompted that decision.

Proactive decision needs arise as a way to set and drive policies. These needs arise in strategy review sessions in which the organization sets/revisits its purpose, vision, mission, and plan, or on an ad-hoc basis as needed. During strategic reviews we recheck the strategic intent, assess the environment, assess our standing and progress, and look for warning signs (e.g., a reduction in subscriber renewals that can signal a market shift). Proactive events generate decision needs that cascade down from the strategy layer to the execution layer—a change in strategy has to be incorporated in the capacity which reflects in scheduling and finally in the day-to-day execution.

Reactive decision needs arise when your alarm system flags an alert. Such alerts drive decisions that constantly align execution to policy. These decisions have to be made fast so as to not impede execution and their effects can migrate up the decision-making stack from the execution layer to the strategy layer. We propose that all such decision needs should be addressed first in the Control Systems layer to enable speed as well as strategic alignment. For example a large batch of goods in a factory is rejected and has to be reworked, which changes the schedule for the impacted factory and the ripple spreads to other factories that must re-plan, and then the impact on the revenue and margin projections at the strategy level has to be re-assessed.

Adaptive decision needs refer to the ability of an organization to sense external and unexpected events and to incorporate their effects adaptively. These events are of diverse nature: a huge tsunami hits Japan, a new tax law is enacted in China, an influential blog post reviles your customer service, etc. These decision needs are difficult to address, because it may not be apparent as to which decision layers need to respond, or how.

Regardless of the need that prompts a decision, the decision need is propagated through the decision layers. Decisions in higher layers have an impact on operations at the lower decision layers, since decisions at the lower layers are constrained by the decisions made that the higher layers. Similarly, decisions made at the lower layers are propagated upwards for consideration in making subsequent decisions. The interplay between decision needs and decision layers is illustrated below (Fig. 2.2).

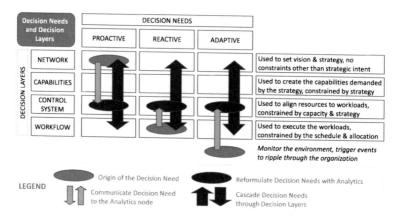

Fig. 2.2 Decision layers and decision needs

This formulation of decision needs is an evolution of Systems 3, 4, and 5 in the Viable System Model[1] proposed by Stafford Beer: System 3 that performs internal monitoring and coordination, System 4 that senses the external environment and assesses what changes are needed, and System 5 that is used to set strategy and policies for the organization. In our formulation, all three Systems share the same analytical model that aligns strategy, planning, control and execution at the Control Systems Layer that provides for the required level of detail and variety.

The decision framework laid out in this chapter is applicable at all the four decision layers, and identifying the layer of decision need origination is the critical first step in leveraging the framework. We will discuss the details of each of the analytics domain functions and their relationship to the decision layer in detail in subsequent chapters, but it is essential that the reader understand the concepts of decision layers before diving into the implementation of the analytics domain functions.

Models: Connecting Decision Needs to Analytics

Reality is complex, and cause-effect chains are intricately networked. To address the need for rational decisions, we create "model" to help us arrive at the best decisions. These models incorporate selected aspects and perspectives of the problem—the model needs to be as simple as possible and only have as much complexity as is required to help make the decision.

Network models are used to make decisions that connect market or ecosystem needs to the workflows and capabilities required to address the need. Such models address aspects such as products (new product introduction, end-of-life, refresh, etc.), customers (segmentation, lifetime value, attrition, retention, etc.) distribution channels, and pricing. The focus is on finding and addressing market needs to achieve strategic goals such as profit, revenue, breadth-of-service, etc. Such models are used when the Decision Need has its roots in the Network Layer. The ecosystem typically consists of entities that are engaged in an end-to-end business process.[2]

Capability models are "introspective" in that, they seek to assist decisions internal to the organization. Such models treat market and business constraints as a "given". These models are used to run, set-up, or evolve the capability in line with the business needs, and focus on efficient design and operation. Examples include product delivery capabilities (factories, warehouses, supply-chains etc.), service delivery capabilities, manpower planning, customer facing capabilities, offering design and development (R&D) capabilities, etc. These types of models serve a Decision Need originating in the Capability Layer.

---

[1] http://en.wikipedia.org/wiki/Viable_system_model.

[2] Brache AP and Rummler GA (1990) Improving performance: how to manage the white space on the organization chart. Jossey-Bass, San Francisco

Control Systems models address the need to change, and they come in these types:

1. Optimization Systems Models are used where we can design, build, execute and trust the analytics required to make optimal choices. In operation, these models are often semi-automated and may even be fully automated.
2. Value Improvement Models are used when we can build analyses and compare options but it is not possible to definitively optimize the recommendations. These models enable the search for options, learning by modeling, comparing options, and learning in the modeling process.
3. Learning-by-Experiment Models are used to systematically improve by the process of experimentation. One process is to run controlled experiments in which we scientifically design and conduct experiments. In the second, we use the naturally occurring diversity around us to serve as "natural experiments" that we can analyze. In both cases we must leverage the results to continuously improve.
4. Learning-by-Asking Models are survey or feedback instruments that are used to guide decision making.
5. Expertise Models are used to learn from the history of input, decision, and outcome data records to help guide current decisions. In many cases, this learning model can be encoded in machine-learning algorithms.

Workflow models are used to observe and govern processes, manage dispatch, and generate alerts.

What is interesting in such a classification of models is that on first glance they share a lot of commonality. For instance, a Pricing model could potentially be classified under any of the four layers listed above. Why then, this attempt at classifying models? On deeper inspection, it becomes clear that the *objectives* or decisions driven by the model are, in fact very different. This difference stems from the Decision Layer where the Decision Need originated.

- Pricing as an "Ecosystem Model" provides pricing answers: "How will my market-share shift with a price movement?" "How will a price position affect my Brand position?" "What kind of response can I anticipate from the competition to my price move?" "How much of a demand/revenue lift can I expect for a given price move?" This is the view from outside—Pricing as a "black box".
- Pricing in the "Capability Model" would address a very different set of questions: "Do we have the resources to build, operate, and evolve pricing models for the organization?" "What does it cost for us to have a pricing capability?" This is the view taken from the inside—Pricing as a "white box" set of people, tools, and methods, who require offices, computers, electricity, coffee, etc.
- Pricing in the "Control Systems Model" would be used to design and monitor the pricing capability. This is the view taken by the analytics practitioner who is building the "brains" of the organization to help it think and evolve systematically.

- Pricing in the "Workflow Model" would be used to provide prices to customers within the process of making the sale, and recording if the result was a sale-closed, lost, or negotiated-down.

What is critical is that "Pricing models" have varying levels of complexity, methodology and data needs depending on which decision layer each resides in, which in turn is governed by the layer in which the Decision Need originated. An understanding of the decision layers then becomes an essential aspect of building a model that is appropriate to the needs that it seeks to address. More often than not, excellent models are discarded or disregarded owing to a fundamental disconnect in understanding the layer of play.

Stakeholders

Decisions will directly affect some people, and ripple through to affect others. These people (e.g., employees, suppliers, distributors, customers, etc.) collectively represent the stakeholders in the decision. All stakeholders may not be directly involved in the decision making process, but we need to take care to include them. In many cases, if we don't consider these stakeholders we may be unable to execute the decision. These stakeholders may ask "what's in it for me?" and refuse to act in alignment with the decision if they do not perceive their interests are taken into consideration.

The people who make and execute decisions are the most visible stakeholders in the decision making process. These stakeholders carry the responsibility of rational decision making, and need to prepare themselves for their role. However, help is at hand and they can call upon the support structure of "advisors" or "helpers" to assist them.

Those who help or advise in the decision making process often belong to staff organizations such as IT or analytics. They carry the responsibility of developing the capabilities needed to provide effective assistance to the decision makers. People filling this need are generally referred to as "Business Analysts" in most organizations today, but often lose sight of the advisory role they are supposed to play.

Roles: Connecting Stakeholders to Analytics

As outlined above, there are three roles in decision making: decision maker, advisor, and analyst.

Decision maker: the responsibility and accountability for rational decision making rests with the "decision maker" who is expected to take decisions and also to drive the culture of rational decision making. This "decision maker" is a leader, because with leadership comes the responsibility to own and make the decisions for the organization's direction, strategy, and day-to-day execution. Leaders may autocratically make the decisions themselves or democratically enable a set of people to come to a decision, but this is a matter of leadership structure, and does not dilute the leader's responsibility and accountability for rational decision making.

Decision-making roles are often shared between different people, so as to improve the quality of the decision, improve buy-in, or as a system of checks and balances.

Advisor: in many organizations, the "decision maker" or "leader" is provided with advice to help her/him come to a rational decision. We use the term "advisor" to denote the role of the person or team that provides the advice.

Splitting the role of advisor across different teams generally results in clashing analyses: e.g., the Sales and Finance departments may come up with different analyses to measure the return on a sales campaign. It is best to make it the role of one advisor to incorporate different perspectives within a single decision making context.

Analyst: advisors can be supported by a set of analysts who work with the advisor, or conduct the analysis on their own. Analysts can support the advisor, or the advisor can be an analyst too (the same person can play both roles).

The analyst role is often split across organizations such as analytics, IT and staff organizations such as Operations teams, and with good effect, as it enables focus and cultivates technical depth in different analytics functions. This depth can be leveraged by the advisor, and is often needed. Analysts can balance their depth and breadth based on exposure, experience, and education, possibly leading up to deeper expertise as analysts, to advisory roles, or to decision-making positions in staff or line-of-business teams.

Chapter 3
Decision Framing: Defining the Decision Need

In this function, we define and articulate the decision need in a form and structure that enables effective modeling. An effective decision frame will guide the modeler to build, test and validate appropriate models, guide rational decision making and identify ways and means of measuring and controlling outcomes. To achieve this we need a clear understanding of the decision need and the organizational capabilities to execute decisions that satisfy the decision need. This step also establishes the size and scope of subsequent analysis. Poor framing can doom any analytics to failure.

Big Y, Little Y and Decision Framing

A notion that readers may be familiar with is the notion of the Big Y and the Little Y. These are notions that were popularized by the Six Sigma methodology of process improvement.

*In Six Sigma terminology, **Big Y** refers to the important high level measure that Six Sigma seeks to improve. This Big Y is often broken down into several operational **Little Y**, or operational measures that need to be improved in order to improve the Big Y*

In this context, the Decision Framing function can be seen as clearly defining the Big Y. It is a common error of omission where the Decision Frame articulates a Little Y, while the stakeholders are looking closely at a Big Y. It is sometimes appropriate that a Decision Model is required in the context of a Little Y (In fact, it is not uncommon to have a series of decision models to address different Little Y, that are collectively used to improve the Big Y). The confusion arises when a model is presented that addresses a Little Y and that is not articulated clearly.

In such a situation, a Decision Frame is established for the Big Y and multiple Decision Frames for each of the Little Y. Care should be exercised in communicating Decision Model output to emphasize the specific Decision Frame that the model addresses and how it fits into the Big Y scheme.

R. Saxena and A. Srinivasan, *Business Analytics*, International Series in Operations Research & Management Science 186, DOI: 10.1007/978-1-4614-6080-0_3,
© Springer Science+Business Media New York 2013

Decision frames are by no means static, and can evolve iteratively based on assessing the decision model, observing the outcome of decision execution and providing feedback to the decision frame (Fig 3.1).

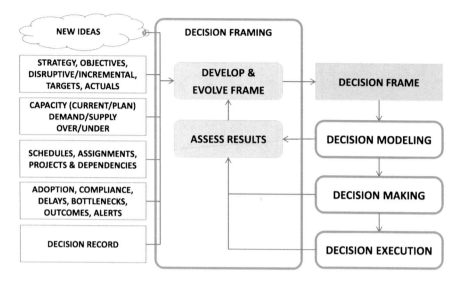

Fig. 3.1 Decision framing

We start by understanding the current state and the Decision Need. This is achieved by a clear articulation of the purpose of the Decision Need and the environment in which the need will be met (through a Decision). In addition, a thorough understanding of the capabilities (current and future) and processes to enable the organization to execute on the decision is critical. This remains another point of failure of analytics when capabilities and processes are not geared to handle the recommendations of the Decision Model.

> At a meeting of the marketing planning department, it was decided to leverage analytics to increase the returns on Direct Marketing Campaigns. To this end, a lot of thought was given to the desired outcome and a very clearly articulated Decision Frame was established. A Decision Model was demanded that could predict the "Next Likely Purchase" of an existing customer and use this model to roll out a customized offer by e-mail to encourage the customer to buy.
>
> A Model was designed that analyzed the purchasing patterns of all existing customers and predicted the probability that a given customer would buy a specified product within the next 3 months. Part of the model parameters included customer specific demographic information.

> *Everything was in order, a clearly articulated Decision Need, well structured Decision Frame and a well designed Model. However, for the model to evolve and improve, it is required to track the performance of these customized offers to understand the effectiveness of the model and improve over time.*
>
> *Unfortunately, prevalent processes and technologies did not capture the customer's response after an offer was made (All customers who received similar offers were directed to a common web page to complete their transaction). Consequently, the system could not provide feed-back to the model the exact outcome of the offer made to a specified customer. This meant that the learning loop of the model was compromised and the entire project had to be put in "cold storage" till the ability to track individual customer's response was made available.*
>
> *Failure to understand the capabilities and processes needed to implement the Decision Model necessitated an undue delay in the roll out of the model.*

To effectively frame the Decision Need, one needs to think about and frame the problem in terms of

1. Purpose and objectives—what is the decision need that triggered the decision modeling requirement
2. Context—the decision layer in which the need originated
3. Scope and Constraints—what is off-limits for changes and recommendations
4. Envisioned end state—a "virtual" walk through that can articulate the end state that is the desired outcome of the decision making process
5. Organizational structure, systems, and culture
6. Risks—including the risk of non-execution of the analytical model

In addition to clearly stating the Decision need, Decision Framing also guides the modeler or Analyst towards the right Decision Model. This is an extremely important facet especially for optimization models, where the complexity and tractability of the model are driven by the complexity of the constraints that are imposed on the problem.

Example 1: A statement like *"Which customers should I make a special offer so that I get maximum returns (Sales) for minimum cost?"* is an example of a badly framed decision need. Say that this need is to help a set of call center agents in the "Execute" decision layer to determine whether to make an offer, and will either be enacted as a policy or as the output of an analytical tool embedded in the workflow system. It is framed badly because it is not clear to the modeler if the decision criterion is increased sales or lower costs. A better way to frame the need is *"Which customers should I make a special offer so that I can maximize sales and my cost does not exceed $X?"*

Example 2: Airlines have to assign each arriving and departing flight to a gate to board and disembark passengers. A decision need that was placed on the Analyst was to develop a model that would help a planner decide which flight to assign to which gate so that the total gate usage was minimized and all flights were gated. While this statement is very clear about the decision need, it is not complete without a few additional requirements. There is a physical constraint – some gates that cannot take certain types of aircraft (Gate too small, too low, etc.). Now, this places a constraint on the model and it is critical for the decision need to be framed to include this fact otherwise there is nothing to prevent the model from suggesting a gate assignment that is not workable. This is an example where a physical "walk through" of the gates would be needed to provide the analyst with the physical context for the decision need and avoid downstream aggravation.

Decision Framing for Decision Layers

Decision Framing establishes the purpose, approach, and constraints that the decision modeling step requires. Decision Frames are born from decision needs and as we saw in the previous chapter, decision needs come in unique flavors depending on the decision layer that the need arises in. Decision Frames in essence capture the decision layer where the decision need arose. It is then logical to assume that Decision Frames retain the unique flavors of layer that triggered the decision need and have their own corresponding characteristics (Fig 3.2).

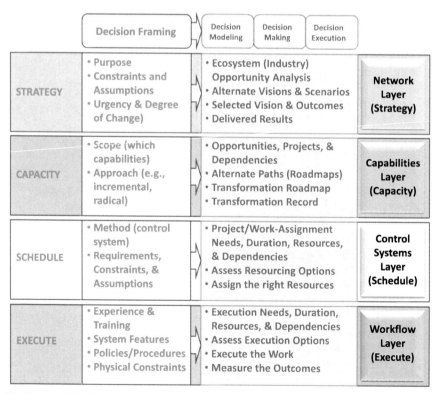

Fig. 3.2 Decision frames and layers

The Airline Partnership Model

Commercial airlines have long established partnership agreements (known as code-share agreements) in order to expand their market reach.

A code share agreement is essentially a partnership agreement between two airlines that allows one airline (the marketing carrier) to sell a ticket on the partner (operating airline) operated flight, as its own flight. This should be very familiar to readers who have booked tickets (esp. international travel) with an airline that says "operated by xyz airline" on the ticket.

For example, a major European carrier operates flights to most European destinations from its central Hub, but only flies to a limited set of US destinations (Gateways). European passengers desirous of travelling to an alternate US destination will have to fly to the US gateway, and travel on another airline to get to their eventual destination. The carrier can choose to expand its operation to second tier destinations in the US, or partner with a US carrier to sell tickets to these alternate destinations that will be carried by the partner.

Such agreements are very commonplace in the industry, and in fact, have expanded to form "Global Alliances" like One World, Star Alliance etc. comprising of multiple carriers worldwide to ensure global reach of each partner airline.

We will use this example all through this chapter to illustrate the various decisions that are called for in such a scenario, and illustrate the different Decision layers and Decision Frames that come into play.

Network Layer (Strategy)

Decisions frames at this layer focus on addressing decision needs of the organization as it pertains to the environment that it operates in. The characteristics of the decision frames at this layer mirror the characteristics of the decision needs that they serve. For instance, these decision needs tend to be very "loosely" defined. There are few, if any, constraints on the model. As these decisions tend to have long lasting and deep impact they are not taken lightly. Decision frames at this layer invariably spark other decision frames (possibly at other layers) that trigger their own analytics framework – See the example on the Big Y/Little Y introduced in the previous chapter. The interesting aspect of decision frames at this layer is that, while they tend to be minimally constrained, they impose constraints on the decision frames that originate in other layers. A capability decision frame, for instance has to be subjugated to Network (strategic) decision frame to ensure that the various decisions are not opposed to each other.

Purpose and Objectives are typically drawn from strategic and long term goals of the organization, so we often find that decision needs tend to be more growth focused (decisions for revenue improvement, as opposed to cost reduction). Constraints are few, if any, and typically, the decision model will be called upon to evaluate various constraints. Organizational structure, processes and culture play dominant roles in decision frames at this layer.

The Airline Partnership Model: Phase 1

Continuing our discussion on the Airline Partnership Model, we can see how a Network Decision Frame is used to trigger critical decisions on partnerships.

The decision need arises from the objective of an airline to grow its revenues by expanding into newer markets. As an airline grows its network, it reaches a point of diminishing returns, where newer markets become increasingly difficult to open up. In addition, regulatory constraints limit the choice of markets that an airline can serve. For instance, an airline may not provide carriageway for passengers between two points, both of which are outside of the carrier's home country, i.e., a US carrier may not serve a market that is entirely within Europe.

As in the previous illustration, we consider a European carrier that flies from its Hub in Europe into key gateways in the US. The carrier is keen on offering its customer's services to other US destinations and would like to do so in partnership with a US domestic carrier.

The Decision frame in this scenario would be a simple statement of a need to identify the best set of Partner airlines and newer destinations served. In some cases, when the airline is part of a global alliance (Star Alliance, One World etc.) the choice of partner may be limited to a fellow member of the alliance, in which case the decision frame reduces to identifying the best set of destinations to bring into the partnership framework. This will create a decision model to identify, evaluate and recommend destinations in the partner network that best meet the airlines objective.

Capability Layer (Capacity)

In the capability layer, the decision frame will focus on determining the best capabilities of the organization that is aligned to the decisions made at the network layer. A company generally consists of a set of capabilities, where a specific instance of a capability could be swapped-out with another of the same type, to improve its performance in the context of the organization's performance in the network. For example, we can focus on calculating the optimal size for a manufacturing cell (capability) and the number and location of these cells so that they work effectively in the supply network.

Decision frames at this layer are invariably constrained by decisions made at the Network layer. For instance, a decision need that addresses the number of service agents to staff in a support contact center would be framed at this layer, but is constrained by decisions made at the network layer viz.

- Location of the contact center
- Committed SLA (average waiting time, specialty queues, premium queues etc.)
- Insourced/Outsourced agents

In more evolved organizations, Decision frames at the Capability layer are defined and used as inputs to the decision frame at the Network layer.

The Airline Partnership Model: Phase 2

Continuing our discussion on the Airline Partnership Model, we can see how a Capability Decision Frame is used to operationalize the partnership decisions taken at the Network Layer.

The decision need arises from the objective of an airline to execute on its partnership decision. The choice of partner and destinations has been made at the Network layer, and the decision need here is to identify specific flights within the partner network that will be tagged with "Codeshares". The decisions at this layer are limited to choosing such flights and determining the available capacity on these flights (reserved for codeshares). This kind of capacity decision is known as a "hard block" in the airline industry and refers to the situation where the marketing airline reserves a fixed number of seats on the operational flight for its exclusive use.

This decision frame will institute a Decision Model that will choose the best set of flights and capacities from the list of partner flights that will maximize the airlines ability to serve newer destinations and capture revenue. The details of the model are not pertinent to this discussion, but suffice it to say that the expected output of the model is a list of partner flights and required capacities. In some cases, the model may be expected to suggest a "price" at which the capacity should be purchased or a "bid value" for the capacity. If the price of the capacity is determined a priori (in the Network layer), it is simply fed as a constraint into the decision model here.

Control Systems Layer (Schedule)

In the Control Systems layer, the decision frame will focus on optimizing utilization of capabilities that are set based on decisions made at the capability layer. Decision frames at this layer are peppered with various operational constraints that are unique to the organization and sometimes even the business unit within the organization. Decision frames at this layer are reused several times (by design). Decisions are made for a limited scope, and a frame is reused upon expiry of that scope.

For instance, a staffing decision can be made for a set of tasks that need to be completed. This decision will be based on a decision model that makes the optimal recommendations based on certain input parameters (demand for tasks, duration of tasks, availability of resources etc.). When any of these parameters change substantially, the model will be required to re-evaluate and recommend (possibly) alternate decisions. Such dynamic changes to recommendations can be extremely cumbersome to handle, and hence decision frames at this layer typically limit the scope of validity of these recommendations (For the next week, for the next 100 orders etc.). Upon expiry of the scope, the model is reused using more current and up-to-date data. Literature is rich with cases of such decision frames and models, and in cases where such limiting of scope is unacceptable; the model is used to generate rules that are passed on to the Workflow layer to be executed (Fraud prevention is a classic example).

The Airline Partnership Model: Phase 3

At this stage of the Airline Partnership Model, we can see how a Control System Decision Frame is used to optimize the capabilities created in the Capabilities Layer.

The decision need arises from the objective of the airline to utilize the new capabilities (new destinations, and additional capacity) to generate additional revenue and provide better services to its customers. The choice of partner, destinations and flights has been made at the higher layers, and the decision need here is to identify the necessary capacity on the partner flights and the appropriate pricing of tickets that use that capacity.

This decision frame will institute a Decision Model that will determine the optimal pricing and the necessary capacity to be made available in any given market. The model will be required to consider market dynamics, competitive options, price elasticity of the market and other various factors to recommend the optimal combination of capacity and price. The model will take as input some constraints inherited from the previous layers that determine that the available capacity for purchase cannot exceed x, or the bid price for the capacity cannot be below y (based on the exact text of the partnership agreement)

Where this gets really interesting, is that, the Decision Model may return a trivial solution of NOT choosing any capacity for a destination. This could occur if the constraints inherited from the previous layers are too binding.

For instance, the market dynamics dictate that the pricing in the market will have to be very low, but the minimum bid price is set very high. In such cases, the Control System effectively negates the decisions from the higher layers. We will look at how such situations can be avoided in subsequent examples

Workflow Layer (Execute)

In the Workflow layer the organization executes its work—assigning tasks to people or machines, providing the workflows and procedures to do the work, accepting or rejecting a booking request, and setting up events and alerts to monitor the workflow.

Instrumenting and acting in this layer brings us into the world of "real time" analytics. To avoid getting caught up into what it means to be "real time" we prefer to name it inline analytics that operate within the timing requirements required by the business process, as opposed to offline analytics that cannot execute in line with the workflow but get used in the other offline layers (schedule, capacity, and strategy).

The Airline Partnership Model: Phase 4

At this stage of the Airline Partnership Model, we simply choose to accept or reject a booking request from a passenger based on the willingness to pay. For instance, when a passenger requests a ticket to travel to one of the destinations serviced by the partnership arrangement, we can offer the partner flight combination as a possible choice. If the choice is attractive to the customer, a sale is made. However, since the sale of this ticket excludes the sale of alternate tickets to different passengers, to different destinations (that share the common flight from the European Hub to the US Gateway), the shared resource will be offered to the highest bidder. What this means is that a Control System decision of capacity may never be used since the market pricing for the destination is unviable.

Let us illustrate that further. The Airline operates a flight from the European Hub (called EUH) to a US Gateway (called USG). A passenger can travel from EUH to USG, and then connect on to several flights (Other carrier, our Codeshare etc.) to various destinations. If only one seat is available on the EUH-USG flight, and 2 passengers, one travelling to Destination DES1 and the other travelling to destination DES2 request a ticket, we can sell only one of them since both are competing for the single available seat on the EUH-USG flight. Our decision frame will choose the passenger such that the revenue generated is maximized (the highest bidder for the single seat). It is immaterial to the decision frame here that the flight to DES1 is, in fact, a codeshare flight while the flight to DES2 is not. All that matters at this decision layer is selecting the passenger such that the total revenue generated for the airline (from EUH-USG-DES1 in the first case, and EUH-USG only in the second) is maximized. If the EUH-DES1 market is a weak market that cannot bear a high price, no tickets will be sold on the Codeshare flight.

The Execute layer decision has essentially made the entire set of decisions leading up to this null and void!

Aligning the Layers: Tying the Decision Frame

The Example running through the previous section illustrated how Decision Frames at various layers can work against each other unless they are aligned. This is easier said than done. The first trap that organizations fall into is having different departments that focus on different decision layers. This is the root of the problem that is highlighted eloquently as a "Failure to Embrace Analytics" in the decision making process. Not understanding the interplay between these layers is the reason why some organizations' tentative steps to be analytically oriented fail, since the Analytical capabilities are concentrated in one of the layers (Usually the lower two) and cannot truly permeate all layers.

The key to leveraging this understanding of the layers of decision framing is to establish a robust feedback loop between the layers. Essentially the Decision Frame at any layer has to create decision needs at the lower layers and use the feedback from the lower layers as constraints for the decision frame.

The ability to build effective decision models depends on the ability to articulate needs and constraints and on the quantity and quality of data available to drive these decision models. The quality and quantity of available data increases at the lower layers (more operational and transactional) and it stands to reason that decision models are best pushed to the Control Systems layer that can leverage all that data without running into the decision constraints and response-time requirements of Workflow layer analytics that limit model complexity in this lowest layer.

The sweet spot of leveraging analytical capabilities occurs in the Control System Layer. Let us pause to reflect on the nature of this layer that allows us to make this assertion:

- Data availability is of sufficient quality and quantity to support Decision Models.
- The Decision Models can exist "Offline"
- Constraints from just one layer below are not overwhelming
- Decision modelDecision models from higher layers can be translated into decision needs at this layer without unnecessary complexity.
- Decisions at this layer are easily translated into rules to be embedded into the inline decision making systems at the Workflow layer

What this means is that one has to be very careful in structuring the analytics teams that drive the organizational analytical competence. It does not make sense to position your analytics teams outside the CEO's office in the warped idea that visibility and support from the executives is going to enable success. Similarly, it makes no sense to position analytics teams at the execution level (the customer support team for instance).

As analytics teams are being set up, they should be focused on building capabilities that can be consumed at the Control System layer. The higher layers should set up liaison functions that can talk to these analytics teams and articulate decision needs and decision frames.

Decision Frames Set Business Expectations

Think of decision framing as the key function used to set expectations about what the analytics will deliver. It can literally be compared to the sales function, that front-ends any future development, delivery and operation of analytics. Set expectations correctly and you set the analytics initiatives on a path to success.

As one progresses through the process of using the decision frame to build models and guide decision making, it is easy to lose track of the problem that sparked the decision need in the first place. The decision frame will be constantly revisited and refined through the entire life of the analytics exercise. Constant communication with the business stakeholders is essential to ensure that the decision frame is set correctly.

Just as the decision frame guides the decision model, it also is used to evaluate and pass judgment on the quality of the resulting model. Decision models lose context in isolation and can be been seen for their true worth only in the context of the decision frame that defined the necessary model.

In that regard, decision frames play a very critical role of setting business expectations on the resulting model. It is extremely important for the analyst to "carry" the decision frame through the entire life of the decision model, and communicate that clearly to the stakeholders to set their expectations on what to expect (and sometimes, what NOT to) from the decision model. We will cover some aspects of setting the context and business expectations in subsequent chapters in this book.

Chapter 4
Decision Modeling

A model is an abstraction of reality or a representation of a real object or situation. A model presents a simplified version of reality—it may be as simple as a drawing of house plans, or as complicated as a miniature but functional representation of a complex piece of machinery.

"All models are wrong, but some are useful"
—George E. P. Box in the *Journal of the American Statistical Association* 71:791–799 (1976)

For business analytics, a decision model is an abstraction that shows key variables and relationships. We use models to learn about their real-life counterparts. We judge how well a model corresponds with reality by manipulating its variables and observing the results, and then we use it as a proxy for the complex reality—a useful proxy that can be used to generate insights and optimal decisions. A model must eliminate unimportant details (it has to leave out the plethora of variables we encounter in our complex real world) and focuses on the decision variables relevant to a situation. This focus helps people to better understand the issues, courses of actions, and outcomes. Since they are simplified simulations of reality, models are easier to use and less expensive than dealing with the actual situation and also enable us to explore "what-if" scenarios that vary the situation to assess the results of different inputs and changing assumptions.

In the context of our Analytics Domain, a decision model stems from the decision frame that has been established. We can build, test, iterate and evolve the decision model. The process of building the model is often broken into sub-steps such as Formulation, Data Collection, Development, Testing, Evolution, and Presentation (Fig. 4.1).

R. Saxena and A. Srinivasan, *Business Analytics*, International Series in Operations Research & Management Science 186, DOI: 10.1007/978-1-4614-6080-0_4, © Springer Science+Business Media New York 2013

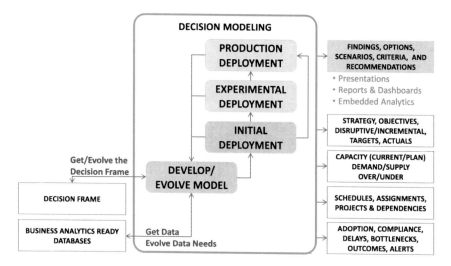

Fig. 4.1 Decision modeling

Types of Models

When we choose to represent reality with a model, it falls upon the modeler to identify the parameters that are relevant and provide a truthful representation of reality in the context of use of the model. As one may well imagine, modelers have evolved several modeling techniques over the years, that are best suited to develop relevant models to the context that they operated in. Models however, are not a figment of a modeler's imagination as one may presume, but are usually built upon a thorough understanding of the reality and an appreciation of the various techniques at the modeler's disposal.

> It is a capital mistake to theorize before you have all the evidence. It biases the judgment.
> —Sherlock Holmes, a *fictional* character
> Some scientists find, or so it seems, that they get their best ideas when smoking; others by drinking coffee or whisky. Thus there is no reason why I should not admit that some may get their ideas by observing, or by repeating observations.
> —Sir Karl Popper, in *Realism and the Aim of Science* (1983)

While the earlier chapters tried to empower the reader with techniques to foster a better understanding of reality and context, here we try to provide the reader with a variety of models and techniques that have been used successfully, and encourage the reader to think of various contexts within the framework of these models.

These models and techniques are by no means exhaustive, nor are they meant to be. The reader is encouraged to identify more models and patterns in their experience and add to this reference list (Fig. 4.2).

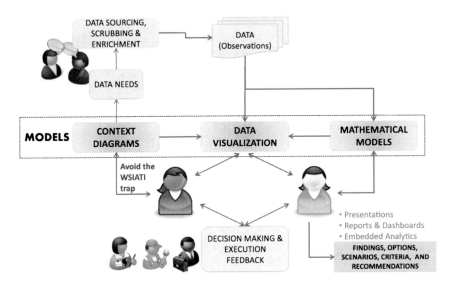

Fig. 4.2 Types of models

Context Diagrams

These are "boxes and arrows" kinds of pictures. This book is peppered with them, and you'll find them used in the fields of process mapping, business architecture, management, and systems design. These models are very useful to think about the problem space and scope, to understand the various elements that make up the problem space and the interplay between them. Armed with this information, the analyst can build a concept about how to characterize and address the problem. These diagrams are used to come to a common understanding of the scope and concerns for the analysis in collaboration with decision makers and decision execution teams. They are also used to generate the data needs and to help data providers think about how to get the right data for the analysis. These conversations and iterations lead to a shared understanding. They also help us avoid the error of "What You See Is All There Is"[1] (WYSIATI)—an amalgamation of confirmation bias, jumping to conclusions, and tunnel vision.

A special mention needs to be made of *metaphors*, which are a special class of context diagrams that paint a "verbal" picture to describe the context by drawing a parallel to a picture that the audience would be familiar with. However, since a key consideration of a context diagram is to generate engagement and conversation, metaphors are best avoided while making these diagrams, as people react to

---

[1] Kahneman D (2011) Thinking, fast and slow. Allen Lane, London.

metaphors and stories in ways that can distract them from the subject. Metaphors and stories have a place—they make for memorable and impactful communication—but if our intent is to foster productive debate and conversation then they can be derailing.

Data Visualization

Built upon the adage that "A picture is worth a thousand words", data visualization is used extensively to look at the data to find patterns, spot exceptions, deviations and opportunities.

Data visualization has deep roots[2] and famous practitioners such as Edward Tufte and Hans Rosling. Data visualization models often exist in conjunction with other types of models and are usually the most effective medium of communication of model results. Visualization models are also used to set the context of the model and explain the decision frame. We could, in fact, claim without loss of generalization that data visualization models find use in each function of the analytics domain and are necessary to enable a smooth and seamless transition between functions.

We use data visualization models to understand source data using scatter charts, histograms, cross-checks, filters, looking for missing data, etc. Such a model gives us valuable insights into data biases; data quality challenges and guides us on the necessary data stewardship processes that have to be established. Such a model can also be used to assess the effectiveness of data stewardship by applying the model on data before and after the data stewardship loop.

Visualization models are used to guide model developers to the appropriate scale of mathematical models. By enabling dynamic scaling, filtering and clustering, we enable the modeler to easily see and identify patterns in the data (seasonality, end of quarter spikes, trends, natural clusters etc.) that serve as critical input in establishing the right decision frame and the appropriate decision model.

Such models are also used extensively to present the results of your model in a one-time or ongoing basis using graphics to illustrate the analysis. The ongoing use of data visualization for a business is often called a "dashboard". The TED talk by Hans Rosling[3] is a classic use of data visualization in a one-time presentation. You can learn the good and bad cases of examples of visualization

---

[2] Friendly M (2005) Milestones in the history of data visualization: a case study in statistical historiography. In: Classification—the ubiquitous challenge, Part I. Springer, Heidelberg, pp 34–52.

[3] Hans Rosling's TED Talk "*Stats that reshape your world-view*". http://www.ted.com/talks/hans_rosling_shows_the_best_stats_you_ve_ever_seen.html.

in your workplace, in media,[4] and on websites that provide opinions on the subject.[5]

Mathematical Models

These models process the data into a construct that helps people to make sense of the data and use it to guide actions. Mathematical models are often used in conjunction with context diagrams and data visualization to quantify the inter-dependencies between various nodes of a context diagram. In this sense, a mathematical model works with other types of models to drive action, and is often used loosely to represent the entire realm of decision modeling. The area of mathematical modeling is also rich with literature and books that talk about various tools and techniques available to the modeler and it is easy to fall prey to the error of mistaking the trees for the forest. It cannot be emphasized enough that mathematical models are only useful to the extent that the decision frame is established correctly (using appropriate context diagrams) and can be rendered impotent without the use of the right visualization model to illustrate the recommendations of the model.

There are several excellent books[6] on the methods and techniques of mathematical modeling and the bibliography at the end of this book lists several well-known books in these areas. Reference may be made in the following sections to methods such as listed below. While understanding and familiarity of these methods and techniques is not required, the reader is well served to gather a basic understanding of such methods while working through the following sections. A broad sampling of such methods includes:

1. Hypothesis Testing
2. Correlation, Regression, and Forecasting
3. Sampling
4. Control Charts
5. Queuing Theory and Simulation
6. Linear Programming (Simplex)
7. Transportation and Assignment (Simplex)
8. Network Optimization
9. Dynamic Programming
10. Multi-criteria Optimization
11. Project Management with PERT & CPM
12. Inventory Control
13. Dispatch, Scheduling, and Planning

---

[4] http://www.visualizing.org/visualizations.

[5] http://www.datavis.ca/gallery.

[6] For example Hillier FS, Lieberman GJ (2005) Introduction to operations research. McGraw-Hill, Boston or Taha HA (2011) Operations research: an introduction. Prentice Hall, New York.

14. Two-Person, Zero-Sum Games
15. Decision Trees
16. Systems Dynamics
17. Markov chains and Hidden Markov models
18. Bayesian Statistics

Big Data and Big Models

In an increasing number of cases, we see a lot of data has become available to analysts. Modelers get data from financial market trading records, credit card transaction records, retail point-of-sale records, telephone company call data records, log files generated by applications and systems, embedded systems and agents (such as data-loggers in trucks and airplanes, security agents in computers and network devices, RFID readers, etc.), social networking sites such as Facebook and Twitter, video camera feeds, photographs in online repositories, etc. The data stores are huge and becoming larger in volume, we get a torrent of new data at high velocity, and the data comes in a variety of forms (such as log files, Twitter feeds, video, audio, website clickstreams, etc.). In combination, the high volume, velocity and variety of data drive a step change in the way we use data, and this new state of affairs is labeled "Big Data". We use specialized business intelligence systems (such as Apache Hadoop) as well as highly automated data stewardship processes to manage this Big Data.

A similar transformation is occurring in other fields—astronomers, subatomic physicists, and radiologists also use Big Data tools to manage the huge size of the observations they get from telescopes, colliders, and CAT scans.

To leverage Big Data, we deploy Big Models, exemplified by the use of high-frequency algorithmic trading models in financial markets. These models process data and conduct trades at speeds that human traders cannot match.[7] Complex models that leverage large data-sets are used to assess credit card transactions for fraud, to analyze a call-center phone conversation while it is in progress to determine the caller's emotional state, or to continuously monitor a jet engine in flight to determine if it needs service.

The fact that we can create and run these Big Models at speeds that enable the analytics to be used in every transaction makes it possible to eliminate the usual gaps between strategy and execution—a strategy model can now be embedded within a Big Model that drives execution. Analysts at each decision layer can collaborate to make and maintain this model. This presents a grand challenge to the analytics community: to make such integrated big models work (Fig. 4.3).

---

[7] http://en.wikipedia.org/wiki/Algorithmic_trading.

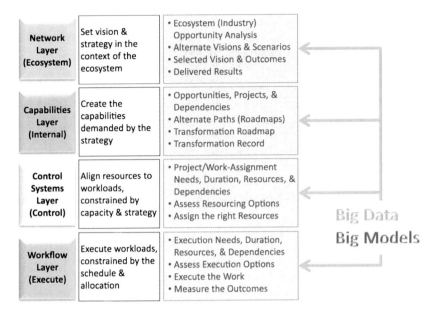

Network Layer (Ecosystem)	Set vision & strategy in the context of the ecosystem	• Ecosystem (Industry) Opportunity Analysis • Alternate Visions & Scenarios • Selected Vision & Outcomes • Delivered Results
Capabilities Layer (Internal)	Create the capabilities demanded by the strategy	• Opportunities, Projects, & Dependencies • Alternate Paths (Roadmaps) • Transformation Roadmap • Transformation Record
Control Systems Layer (Control)	Align resources to workloads, constrained by capacity & strategy	• Project/Work-Assignment Needs, Duration, Resources, & Dependencies • Assess Resourcing Options • Assign the right Resources
Workflow Layer (Execute)	Execute workloads, constrained by the schedule & allocation	• Execution Needs, Duration, Resources, & Dependencies • Assess Execution Options • Execute the Work • Measure the Outcomes

Big Data

Big Models

Fig. 4.3 Big data and big models

In the rest of this chapter we will sketch out examples of models used in the four decision layers.

Network Models

In the network layer the organization exists on cooperation or contention with other entities in its ecosystem. In this domain the analysis focuses in improving the performance of the unit as it interacts with other units. For example a company (unit) serves customer (units) with goods and services in exchange for payments, and our analysis can deal with customer segmentation to increase the company's revenues or optimize pricing to increase the company's margins. At this level, the leadership also sets the required urgency and degree of change, for example by declaring an urgent need to radically transform or a preference for staying the course and incremental changes.

Decision models at this layer are used to set:

- The purpose of the organization. This area is generally the lair of "from the gut" assertions based on deeply held beliefs ... how can "analytics" help?

    - Help people think about possible purposes. People try to link their purpose to a "megatrend" (think: a big opportunity) or to solve a big problem. Analytics is used to define and assess these. The energy industry provides huge opportunities and risks, and several organizations (such as EIA, EPRI, NREL etc.)

devote themselves to providing data and analysis and other analysts use it to further characterize opportunities. Similarly in every industry, analysts and gurus make predictions and identify trends. A recent example is the "Circular Economy" concept from the Ellen MacArthur Foundation.[8] The analyst should also check if a megatrend is a bubble, such as the housing mortgage trend/bubble in the USA[9]—an analyst could check whether price increase trends were justified based on rent-or-buy analysis or the incomes needed to make the mortgage payments for higher-priced homes.

- Size and scope the purpose—it could relate to age or youth, rich or poor, countries or regions, etc. A micro-finance institution would focus on poor countries. An aircraft manufacturer would look at air traffic trends everywhere. Advanced geriatric-care may first seek to address the needs of rich-country populations.
- Identify dependencies upon which the trends hinge. Is the solar panel industry growth dependent on ongoing reductions in the capital cost of the plant (cost per kW)? If so, analysis is needed to assess the effect of the dependency. For instance, large decreases in solar cell cost may translate into much smaller reductions in overall project (plant) cost.

• Creating well-conceived constraints and assumptions is another place where analytics is required. A school's purpose to provide the best education needs to be shaped by a thoughtful consideration of the research on education. A hospital's purpose to provide the best care needs to be founded on the mass of evidence on healthcare needs and delivery.

- Value-chain analysesValue-chain analyses[10] look at revenues and margins at each node in the chain to discover value pools. Analytics is used to look for value-pools within the previous constraints (generally in shares of wallet or degree of penetration) as well as in adjacencies like going upstream (integrating suppliers), downstream (becoming your own distributor or retailer), or sideways (like adding complementary products to your product mix). This exercise often exposes a lack of data—for example a manufacturer with a strong distribution network might consider the value of adding a direct-selling channel, and in doing so discover that they do not know the distributor or retail margin. To revalidate the constraint to remain committed to the channel-selling decision frame an analyst would look at the value pool.
- Healthcare insurance coverage analytics is used to underpin the debate on whether or not the state needs to impose a requirement to buy health insurance.

---

[8] http://www.ellenmacarthurfoundation.org/.

[9] http://en.wikipedia.org/wiki/United_States_housing_bubble.

[10] http://en.wikipedia.org/wiki/Value_chain.

– Sometimes companies embed strategic constraints in their decision frame by pre-selecting their industry positioning,[11] market segment,[12] or value proposition focus (e.g., on product leadership, customer intimacy, or operational excellence).

• Urgency and Degree of Change can be calibrated by analyzing the speed of the trends to model the required scope and speed of change.
  – Kodak needed to change its business model to go from the era of film photography to digital. As it was unable to do so successfully, it went bankrupt. One view is that it was unable to move with the urgency needed.[13]
  – IBM had created a diverse portfolio of businesses but ran into a crisis in 1993. A new CEO was brought in, who moved decisively to execute a turnaround.[14] We could say they moved with well-calibrated urgency.
  – You can also decide on excessive urgency. When many firms in an industry move too fast and overbuild they create a glut. In 2001 the telecommunication industry faced a bust because they overestimated the demand and moved too fast to build capacity.[15]

Example 1: A government agency needs to specify, fund, build, and run a High Speed Rail Corridor. We start by setting the purpose to be the transport of people and goods at high speed … and then have to address the concerns of huge costs, regulatory clearances, the need to get state assistance to help in acquiring land, etc. The project benefits do not outweigh the costs and risks if measured just in terms for higher speed of transport. A recent analysis for a high-speed rail link between Hong Kong and Mainland China[16] included these elements: the social benefit of travel time savings, pollution reduction (from CO_2 and NO_X), improved safety, and increased reliability by avoiding traffic-congestion delays. To get a better picture of the project's benefits, we must model the project to include real estate benefits[17]—the potential to make areas near its route economically more viable, improving the value of land and buildings, and enabling tax-base increases.

Example 2: To develop the strategy and plan for a big data analytics startup that takes data from the "Internet of Things" and moves it via "machine to machine" (M2 M) platforms for analysis, we needed to assess if the M2 M platform provider industry is a supplier or a competitor. To do this, we chalked out the capabilities that our startup needed to become viable and successful, and checked them against the capabilities and strategies expressed by a sample of M2 M companies.

---

[11] http://en.wikipedia.org/wiki/Porter_generic_strategies.

[12] http://en.wikipedia.org/wiki/Blue_Ocean_Strategy.

[13] http://www.forbes.com/sites/johnkotter/2012/05/02/barriers-to-change-the-real-reason-behind-the-kodak-downfall/.

[14] http://hbswk.hbs.edu/archive/3209.html.

[15] http://www.economist.com/node/2098913.

[16] Tao1 R, Liu S, Huang C, Tam CM (2011) Cost-benefit analysis of high-speed rail link between Hong Kong and Mainland China. J Eng Proj Prod Manag 1(1):36–45.

[17] http://knowledge.wharton.upenn.edu/article.cfm?articleid=3062.

The ecosystem is complex by nature: generally its context diagram boundaries are set based on judgments of relevance, and we filter the analyses to focus on aspects such as customers, the supply chain, and the offering lifecycle. The boundaries of the ecosystem under consideration are governed by the decision frame that requires the model. We also have to identify actions of the organization within that ecosystem that we seek recommendations for and the model quantifies the impact of specific actions within the ecosystem.

This layer is characterized by "end to end" process flows that we analyze, monitor, and improve. These processes flow across organization boundaries: sales processes flow across customer, channel-partner, and company boundaries, procurement processes flow between the company and its tiers of suppliers, etc.).

The ecosystem is complex by nature: generally its context diagram boundaries are set based on judgments of relevance, and we filter the analyses to focus on aspects such as customers, the supply chain, and the offering lifecycle. Think of what items pass across the organization boundaries, and within the ecosystem:

- Bookings (contracts) to buy Products and/or Services in exchange for payments or other Products and/or Services.
- Technologies (often embedded in the Goods & Services).
- People (e.g., employees, contract workers, etc.).
- Products and parts.

"PESTLE" is a mnemonic for the elements that can be included in an ecosystem context diagram: Political, Economic, Social, Technological, Legal and Environmental factors. Try to keep the model simple—include only the elements that affect the model in a significant way. Depending on the kind of model we were making, we create a different set of ecosystem boundaries and levels of detail or aggregation:

- For Bookings, we populate the ecosystem depending on the viewpoint for the analysis:
  - For a customer-centric view we include different types of buyers/influencers, different needs, and different buying models. We may categorize our customers by their revenue-size, by their location (country), or by industry.
  - For a distribution chain view, we include customers, channel partners, logistics providers, service providers, and the company
  - For a supply chain view we include our tiers of suppliers in addition to the distribution chain.
  - For a market view we have to model why the target market works. So if you want to analyze the market for heavy trucks you will need to include the overall economy, competing modes of transport, competitors, regulatory moves, your customers' industry, etc.
  - For the financial view of Bookings, Payments and Revenues: creditors, debtors, institutions that extend credit to your customers, process payments, manage currency risk, etc.

- For Technologies we take a technology/product lifecycle view and define the ecosystem to be the company, contract research entities, supply chain partners, as well as the technology providers (such as research universities or IP owning firms), and often include recycling-chain entities.

- For People we need to consider the talent-pools, inflows and outflows from the organization—these include flows from schools into the organization, lateral flows (entries and exits), providers of continuing education, talent pools in different countries, work-permit regulators, etc.

To model the ecosystem, start with a high-level view and progressively zoom in (Fig. 4.4).

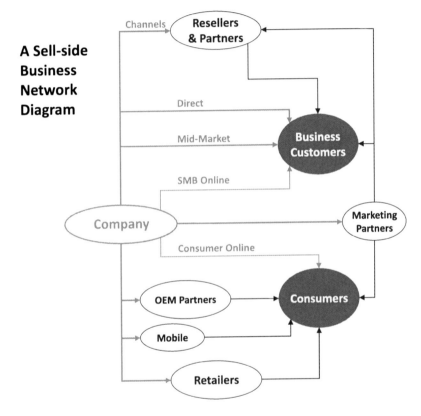

Fig. 4.4 Sell side business network diagram

1. At the top level is a view like the Porter Five Forces[18] model that we use to characterize other entities in the ecosystem as customers, competitors, suppliers, substitutes and potential new entrants. Add "complementors" (or partners of various types) to the list of categories and it becomes a Value Network model. Add countries with their regulations, taxation, and stability if you're modeling globally distributed networks. The idea is to use the categories that

---

[18] http://en.wikipedia.org/wiki/Porter_five_forces_analysis.

make sense or even nested categories if you're modeling a clash of supply-chains or other multi-company networks. At this level you can model how money flows, and who makes what margin.

2. At the next level down, and in successive drill-downs, we need to delve into sub-categories. For instance you could filter for "Mid-Market Customers in China in the Auto Industry" and then analyze market share, margins, installed base, etc. You could keep drilling into this model—e.g., you could keep decomposing that Mid-Market Auto Customer in China from firm to locations (factories), from factories to work-centers to individual machines that use your product. In a similar way, sell-side analyses may drill down to the level of individual people (e.g., buyers or influencers). As entities decompose their functional focus can come into view, so one axis of the drilling will take you into the equivalent of the Porter Value Chain[19] model and then into the different entities involved in a supply chain.

There are different techniques used to drill into the ecosystem context diagrams, and then into the data visualizations and mathematical models. For example:

1. Product Portfolio: funding a portfolio of products in various stages of development, from initiation to end-of-life
2. Customer Portfolio: customer segmentation and market size, addressable market, customer lifetime value
3. Bookings, Revenue, and Margin forecasting and planning, price optimization and discounting
4. Sales and Distribution: sales coverage (assigning sales resources to customers), sales incentives, tracking "opportunity funnels" versus the plan (funnel-snapshot-shape, speed-through-funnel, win/loss and step-conversion rates), partner incentives, sales expenses, etc.
5. Supply Chain: master planning, capacity planning, scheduling and dispatching, sourcing, auctions, products and materials quality, supplier quality, etc.
6. Installed Base: customer-site asset installation status (not installed, installed/deployed, in-service, under repair, feature-usage) cross-sell or up-sell opportunities created by the installed base, usage, maintenance (preventive or on breakdown)
7. Service Supply Chain: services staffing (skills, availability, locations, knowledge-bases, utilization, etc.), services projects and work-orders (to design, install, inspect, maintain, repair and remove/replace), inventory (consumables, spares, and tools for maintenance, repair, and operations), etc.

The data visualization and mathematical models deal with the target market (size, growth rate, penetration, etc.), mechanisms for targeting (such as account coverage, pricing and discounting, cross-sell and upsell), flows through the network (throughput, cycle time, first-pass yield, etc.), industry dynamics (moves made by competitors, suppliers, distributors, etc.) as well as the market results (such as penetration, value created, and value captured).

---

[19] http://en.wikipedia.org/wiki/Value_chain.

Decision Models and the Ecosystem

The definition of the ecosystem by itself can be seen as a context diagram model of the various interdependencies that the organization operates under in the market that it serves. For instance, when we consider the total sales of an organization...

- *We could consider the overall market dynamics that govern the market that the organization operates in (e.g. The current housing market trends if we are looking at selling real estate)*
- *We could look at types of customers, channel partners, distribution network etc. if we are looking at influencing sales through optimal use of supply and distribution chains*
- *We can look at competitive offerings, and segmentation of customers if we are looking at making informed decisions on competitive response to changes in the market*

What is common across these is that the model establishes the question we wish to answer by leveraging specific actions of the organization in response to specific changes to the environment. Given the frame, we build a context diagram model of the various influencers of the decision, and the various nodes that are affected by the decision. Base on this context diagram, we proceed to build mathematical models that quantify the extent of these influences and use that model to make informed decisions on possible courses of action.

For example, the figure below represents a Sell Side Supply chain ecosystem that is defined to understand the dynamics between types of customers and distribution channels. The context diagram clearly identifies possible channel conflicts and allows us to build custom mathematical models that capture the relationships between the nodes and channels.

Capability Models

This layer is characterized and bounded by a focus on creating the set of capabilities required to execute the strategy set in the network layer and to match the capacity with the demand in the most efficient manner. Capabilities include capacities, operational parameters, service-level, quality, skills, technologies etc. that are necessary to execute on the strategy or network decisions.

In the capability layer we work with the "species" that constitute the ecosystem. A company generally consists of a set of capabilities, where a specific instance of a capability could be swapped-out with another of the same type (species) without impact to the company's network (ecosystem). By treating the organization as a set of interacting capabilities, we can focus on a capability to improve its performance in the context of the organization's performance in the network.

For example we can focus on calculating the optimal size for a manufacturing cell (capability) and the number and location of these cells so that they work effectively in the supply network.

Decision models for this layer are used to assess scope, in terms of which capabilities are in or out of scope. Analytics is needed to demarcate the boundary. A factory may need to increase throughput, and analysis is required to locate the bottleneck.[20] A professional services firm may want more resource utilization, and analysis can establish if we need to frame this in terms of optimizing project/task assignments or to also go upstream and see if there will be benefit from smoothing out the demand by creating a backlog of projects that can reduce the feast-and-famine cycles created by starting projects as soon as they are booked and being subjected to the smallest vagaries in the sales cycle.

Capability Models are used to demarcate the scope in terms of diagrams and "building blocks" that stakeholders can understand and agree to. In these models the concept of "capability" is defined differently by different groups of practitioners, but in all cases we arrive at catalogs of capabilities, often arranged hierarchically in a manner foreshadowed by IDEF0.[21] Many consulting firms espouse idea that capabilities combine to create an organization and its ecosystem. Capability Reference Models are catalogs that are in common use in an industry. Examples are:

- APQC Process Classification Framework[22]
- Supply-Chain Operations Reference (SCOR®) model[23]
- Enhanced Telecom Operations Map (eTOM)[24]
- The MIT Process Handbook[25]
- The US government's Federal Enterprise Architecture (FEA)[26]

You must understand the standard capability models available in your industry. In addition, structured techniques such as Solution Envisioning[27] use catalogs of capability cases to help people to envision the capabilities that they can get.

Reference models store knowledge of capabilities and foster reuse: to find a missing or unused capability, benchmark a capability's performance against peers, and select the capabilities to change. In many cases you can buy a capability as a service (e.g., when you can contract with an organization to provide you bookkeeping or logistics planning services), enhance a capability by reusing templates,

---

[20] http://en.wikipedia.org/wiki/Theory_of_Constraints.

[21] http://www.idef.com/IDEF0.htm.

[22] http://www.apqc.org/process-classification-framework.

[23] http://supply-chain.org/scor.

[24] http://www.tmforum.org/BestPracticesStandards/BusinessProcessFramework/1647/Home.html.

[25] http://ccs.mit.edu/phbook.htm.

[26] http://www.whitehouse.gov/omb/e-gov/fea.

[27] Polikoff I, Coyne R, Hodgson R (2005) Capability cases: a solution envisioning approach. Addison-Wesley Professional, Upper Saddle River.

or build by copying. A unique design creates a new entry in the catalog. This happens all the time, and the frameworks stretch to accommodate.

Flow Charts are used to understand how work flows through the capabilities. Analysis of the flows is used to understand the location of bottlenecks, to set up buffers, or to establish controls. We commonly use these types of flow charts:

- Workflow Charts are simple "boxes and arrows" that depict how work flows through steps. Each step may contain a set of steps.
- Cross Functional Flowcharts or swim-lane flowcharts depict how work flows across different people (or teams). The boxes of the Workflow Charts are arranged in lanes, one lane per team.
- In cases where cycle time is important to measure, we can put the elapsed time in an axis for the Workflow Chart or the Cross Functional Flowcharts. Where idle time and work time need to be distinguished, we add a "waiting" box to the flowcharts.

Fishbone diagrams[28] are used to analyze the decision needs and surface areas to study to get to the solution.

Approach (e.g., incremental, radical) specifies the degree of change needed. The methods used in subsequent stages depend upon this assessment. Say that a bank is choosing to build business via call centers instead of adding traditional branch offices—the call center may currently be a cost center that acts as an adjunct to the branch offices and analysis will show what it needs to transform itself into becoming a full-fledged channel. Incremental models are encountered more often, as businesses strive for continuous improvements in productivity. A sales operations team may invest in a case management system to reduce the cycle-time taken to book orders, and analysis determines the approach to be taken—a ramp of continuous small increases, a step change, or a set of steps that will get you to the target.

Example 1: A professional services firm determined to improve its gross margins by improving the utilization of its consultants. A benchmarking study of utilization showed that some other companies got much higher utilization. Capability modeling suggested that a centralized "Resource Management" capability is needed to improve utilization via improved planning, scheduling and dispatch processes. Fishbone diagram analysis pointed us to investigate project time management, and we found that the variance in project time budgets was quite high and also found that the actual time spent does not correlate well to budgeted time. This implied that the scope of the project to improve utilization using Resource Management must also include improvements in Project Management (specifically to improve project time-budgets and schedules) as continued errors in budgeting and time-management would render the Resource Management processes ineffective. Fishbone diagram analysis also showed that we were unable to assess which consultants had the right skills for the task, which also added Skills Management tracking to the project scope.

---

[28] http://en.wikipedia.org/wiki/Fishbone_diagram.

Example 2: A manufacturing firm wanted to develop a business providing services for its customers to maintain the machinery that it sold. To do this, it needed to develop the services capabilities sized to support the business plan. They also wanted to understand how they could use "advanced analytics" to differentiate their services from existing service providers. A fishbone diagram surfaced areas to investigate: spares inventory optimization, predictive maintenance, technician and truck scheduling, etc.

These capabilities are required to be known to the decision models at the network layer, but can actually be specified by custom models that solve for the right capabilities. As we build and evolve network layer models, we use decision models at the capability layer that define what options are available to the network layer model. The network models may, in fact, spawn multiple capability layers that have to work in tandem to effect the best strategic decisions.

Consider the example of the Sell Side business network introduced in the last section. We modeled an organization reaching customer through various channels, partners etc. Under each of the options evaluated in that model, we may choose to leverage capability decision models for a range of capabilities that are necessary. If one were to "peel the layers of the Onion" so to speak, one would find that Marketing and Selling requires several capabilities as shown in the illustration below (Fig. 4.5):

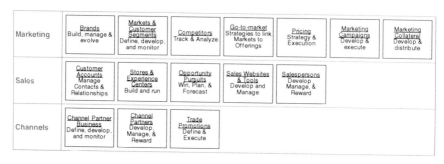

Fig. 4.5 Marketing and selling capabilities

Depending on what was deemed to be in scope at the higher layer, we might need to build models for each of the capabilities listed under Marketing or Sales. Such capabilities exist and are known, and the need for models for these are driven by the scope and frame that allows a change in any capability. For instance, it may be determined that Pricing is not a lever under consideration and hence a pricing capability model may not be called for.

The ability to integrate capabilities into an end-to-end process is also a capability, generally characterized as a backplane, platform, or hub for integration. This capability is characterized by its scope, by operating costs of routing transactions through it (fixed and variable costs), and by the costs of onboarding or removing a capability from the backplane (scaling costs and cycle time). These integration capabilities come in many flavors, such as telecom providers, application service providers, integration middleware systems, electronic data interchange (EDI), etc.

Data visualization and mathematical modeling is used in this layer to model the available capacity and potential, utilization patterns, delivery quality, availability (uptime/downtime, mean time to repair, mean time between failures), adherence to response time, cycle-time and quality service-levels, etc. For example, the number of agents required in a call center determines its capacity, which can be sized based on a queuing model.

Business transformation projects can require a new configuration of capabilities—we may need to add new capabilities, remove old ones, and change some others to align to the transformed business network. The analytics to identify the changes needed include benchmarking and decisions about keeping a capability in-house (build or acquire, sell or shutdown) or to outsource it (rent). The capability transformation model then has to include the cycle time, costs, and talent required to do this.

Control Systems Modeling

Decision needs at this layer are most readily amenable to mathematical modeling and as expected we find the heaviest usage of advanced mathematical modeling techniques such as optimized factory scheduling. As the name indicates, models at this layer borrow from the field of engineering control systems to use a feedback loop to monitor and evolve the decision models based on the outcome of prior period recommendations.

The richness, variety and volume of models at this layer also dictate a sub-classification of models. We present some of the major types of models that are in common use through the industry and the reader is invited to add to and enhance this classification based on his/her experience.

Expertise

In many cases we use our intuition, and in some cases our intuition is honed to expertise by long learning earned in a predictable domain—one that provides clues to guide you to the right course of action, and clear feedback on the outcomes.[29] Examples of predictable domains are chess and nursing, stock-picking is unpredictable. Predictable domains are also amenable to machine learning or checklists,[30] and these mechanisms do not apply intuitive learning inconsistently. Examples are Amazon's Book Recommendation Engine that acts as an experienced bookseller or LinkedIn's 'People

---

[29] Kahneman D, Klein G (2009) Conditions for intuitive expertise: a failure to disagree. Am Psychol 64(6):515–526.

[30] Gawande, A (2009) The checklist manifesto: how to get things right. Metropolitan Books, New York.

You May Know' that works like a matchmaker. Experts are expensive to train and people apply their intuitive judgments inconsistently when they get swayed by extraneous factors, so we can expect machine learning to become more widely used.

Sports such as baseball and football provide a rich record of decisions and outcomes. *Moneyball*[31] is a book and movie that showed the value of using analytics to learn from experience in baseball. Analysis of American football can also be used effectively to guide decisions during games.

The context diagram for an expertise model will list the inputs that the modeler thinks are used to make the expert decision, the output of the decision, and a learning loop to discover the results that enable learning. Mathematical modeling is used to assess how the expert makes decisions (which input variables are used for the decision, in what weights, in which scenarios, etc.), consistency of judgment, accuracy of outcomes (e.g., correct/false positive/false negative, degree of accuracy, etc.). Mathematical modeling can be used to test for evidence whether learning processes improve the accuracy of the expert's judgment by experience.

In cases where the domain is inherently predictable and lends itself to objective judgment we can go on to make a mathematical model for the expert behavior. These mathematical models can be used to "train" themselves to learn how to reason like an expert. Modeling techniques used in this way include Markov chains, regression, and artificial neural networks.[32] In other cases that deal with difficult-to-predict subjects such as stock-picking we could be better off with alternate strategies such as indexing (following the stock index) (Fig. 4.6).

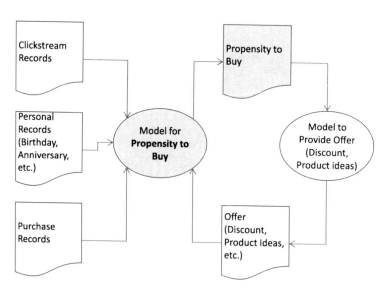

Fig. 4.6 Expertise model

[31] Lewis M (2003) Moneyball. W.W. Norton & Company, New York.

[32] http://en.wikipedia.org/wiki/Machine_learning.

This is the context diagram for an expertise model that assesses a website visitor's propensity to buy. The model itself needs to contain a learning loop to enable it to learn from experience (by examining its prediction of the propensity against the actual purchase records), and also may be composed of a set of models, in two ways:

1. Experiment and Control Models that test new (experimental) models against the current "gold standard" control model
2. Segmented models, where different models are assigned to act on different segments (based on customer profile, product family, website visited, etc.)

We need to continuously monitor the performance of our expertise models to ensure they remain valid or improve over time. To automate the tracking, we can use control charts and alert the analysts if the control limits start to widen as well as with other alerting rules such as successive readings outside the limits on one side, etc. This use of analytics helps analysts avoid the repercussions of obsolete models.

The rate of adoption of analytics for learning is, however, slower than expected.[33] You may be unaware of the analytical approach, or unable to adopt it. James Surowiecki[34] points out that even a professional coach in the Super Bowl did not take advantage of analysis to make key decisions. People often stick to their preferences, tradition, conventional wisdom, or to what they were taught in school without reference to more up-to-date analysis. More often the domain itself may be unpredictable, the number of variables too many, and the outcomes unclear or indeterminate which can make it hard or impossible to build a useful analytical model.

Learning by Asking

This category of models uses statistical surveying,[35] markets[36] or crowdsourcing techniques to get inputs from people. These inputs are used to inform and guide all the analytics functions. This set of methods can be used in many situations, and the aggregate feedback, if credible, provides valuable guidance. Many companies ask their customers for feedback using a survey.

To learn by asking, we need to:

---

[33] Bishop MA, Trout JD (n.d.) 50 years of successful predictive modeling should be enough: lessons for philosophy of science In: Philosophy of science (Proceedings) 68, pp S197–S208.

[34] Surowiecki J (2004) The wisdom of crowds. Anchor, New York, pp 44–48.

[35] http://en.wikipedia.org/wiki/Statistical_survey.

[36] Hoerl AE, Fallin, HK (1974) Reliability of subjective evaluations in a high incentive situation. J Royal Stat Soc 137(2):227–230.

1. Select the people whom we will ask. This selection can be from a list (such as a list of all customers, or filtered to the list of people who bought from us yesterday, etc.), or by enrollment, or from a population (everyone in this shop at this time), etc. Prediction markets and other crowdsourcing techniques get people to form communities of experts who are consulted by the data-gathering instrument.
2. Develop the survey template or data-gathering instrument. This includes deciding on which questions to ask, how to word them, possibly making branching questionnaires or different ones to be used in different cases (either at random or by selection). We also need to decide how to gather data: by sending people out to conduct interviews, as a website-based form, by phone (inbound or outbound), by teleconference, over chat or Facebook, etc. We also determine if we need to record audio and video to add color to the base (text & numeric) responses. The design of prediction markets[37] uses a parallel set of techniques.
3. When the survey is administered, it needs to be set up so that we get the responses from the sample of people we selected to ask. In many cases, the people most interested in answering our survey are the ones most unhappy or very happy, so our response rate contains an over-representation of these populations and under-represents the middling crowd that is not very interested in filling out yet another form. Also, we need to enable the data gathering to elicit honest responses, while recognizing that an honest answer may not fully reflect the actual behavior of the respondent because there is a gap between the way we think we'll act and the way that we actually act. Sometimes, to encourage response rates, we offer rewards (by lottery or guaranteed payments).
4. When survey responses start coming back, we need to review the responses and watch for issues such as spotty or low response rates and misread questions. In many cases we need to remind the selected respondents.
5. The data gathered are visualized and modeled to arrive at results, and to assess the statistical validity and significance of the results.
6. Especially in the case of crowdsourcing, we provide feedback to the respondents about the results and outcomes to enable them to learn by the experience (Fig. 4.7).

When we look at the data visualizations for the survey, we generally see the average response and trends. We should also see the count of responses, the response rates, and in cases where a flow of fresh data is important we should review the flow to see if it departs from previous trends.

The embedded loops in the diagram show an activity to improve response rates and to take action. There needs to also be a separate activity to tie out the survey results against actual behaviors and use that knowledge to improve the survey process.

---

[37] http://en.wikipedia.org/wiki/Prediction_market.

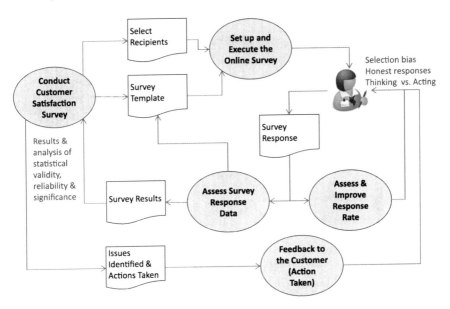

Fig. 4.7 Learning by asking model

Learning by Experiment

In the cases where your company has many similar activities, you can use the experimentation process to assess variations and select the best ones to propagate. This technique applies to finding and evolving the "best practices" for repeated or similar tasks, such as serving hamburgers, offering credit card plans, etc. It also applies to drug testing by pharmaceutical companies, to designing circuits, to improving agricultural productivity, or in patrolling occupied territory.

- Companies use the experimental method to test products such as credit cards[38] or hamburgers before they are launched.
- Clinical trials are structured experiments conducted by pharmaceutical and medical devices companies to assess the effectiveness and side effects of their drugs and devices.
- Evidence-based medicine[39] is used to analyze the track record of various diagnostic tests and treatments to provide guidance on medical decisions.

---

[38] Anderson ET, Simester D (2011) A step-by-step guide to smart business experiments. Harv Bus Rev 89:98.

[39] http://en.wikipedia.org/wiki/Evidence-based_medicine.

- The US Army developed an "After Action Review" method[40] that has also been used by businesses such as British Petroleum and Bechtel.

How can we learn from experiments? At a minimum we need to be able to identify and propagate "winning" variants and avoid less effective ones.

- Controlled Experiments: in this process, the hypotheses are generated, and scientific experiments are designed, run, observed, and analyzed to arrive at conclusions.
- Natural Experiments: this process is used to analyze observations of naturally occurring variants, such as how differences in school attendance can affect earnings later in life, or how variations in management practices in different offices of the same firm drive business results

Controlled Experiments are used by companies to make a wide range of tactical decisions, such as:

- Test changes in website design (deploy the experimental design to a random population of visitors and test if it works better than the existing standard)
- Assess whether a marketing promotion will be effective (deploy the promotion in a random set of stores to see if it pays off) (Fig. 4.8)

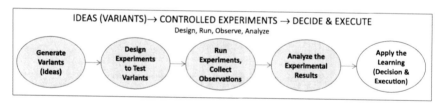

Fig. 4.8 Controlled experiments

Controlled experiments require skills in designing and executing the experiments and in analyzing the results.[41]

1. Generate hypotheses (or variants) by varying selected variables in the target situation (price offered, button placement, etc.). Make a clear definition of the test cases (variants or hypotheses) as compared to the base case (or control)—understand that we get clearer results when there is one (or a few) changes between the test case and the base case, and that correlated variables create noise in the analysis.
2. Design the experiment, with clear definitions to measure variables and outcomes. Experiments use randomized assignments of test-subjects and controls and blind[42] or double blind testing methods.

---

[40] http://en.wikipedia.org/wiki/After_action_review.

[41] Davenport TH (2009) How to design smart business experiments. Harv Bus Rev 69:71.

[42] http://en.wikipedia.org/wiki/Blind_experiment.

3. Run the experiment as designed and record observations objectively. Reject data from experiments that break the protocol.
4. Analyze results and assess validity.

Natural Experiments are used when it is not feasible to make a controlled experiment, for example if we need to assess the lost earnings of a person who became disabled in an accident, or to assess losses inflicted by cartel pricing in a market. In this case, the learning is heavily dependent on the quality of observations and analysis.[43]

The label of "Quasi-experiment" is used where the experiment does not have random assignment of experimental subjects to the treatment or control groups.

Many business situations require the use of natural or quasi experiment analytics techniques. You can use this method to assess the impact of certified project managers on project performance, or to evaluate the business results of using analytics in organizations (Fig. 4.9).

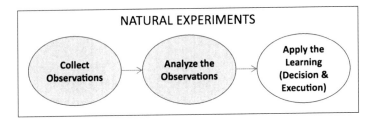

Fig. 4.9 Natural experiments

Value Improvement

This modeling technique is used to design and monitor value improvement roadmaps and analyze the resulting costs, benefits and risks. In this model there is a value improvement cycle that addresses baseline, plan, execute, assess, and adjust elements. Each cycle intends to drive improvement without guarantee that any given cycle will make things better or worse, but over the course of iterations it should work better than an uncontrolled set of activities. Expertise is needed in each step, so each cycle takes weeks or months to go from idea to execution. Many consulting firms have proprietary methods to do this. Businesses commonly establish the agenda for change and drive to the target state by stepping through setting the Target and Baseline States, making a Project Roadmap, and then driving its Governance and execution. We can extend and draw from the experience gained in the manufacturing domain where there are well-established tools and

---

[43] Rosenzweig MR, Wolpin KI (2000) Natural "natural experiments" in economics. J Econ Lit 38(4):827–874.

methods to do this such as Total Quality, Zero Defects, Six Sigma, Lean, etc., that include methods such as

1. Plan-Do-Check-Adjust (PDCA)[44] popularized by Dr. Deming
2. Six Sigma[45] DMAIC, DMADV & DFSS

The generic model for value improvement has three parts:

1. Definition of the Target (Future) State: this includes a description and is characterized with quantitative and qualitative attributes. The future state may be anywhere from one to 5 years distant, depending on the "horizon" used … or series of horizons. These time horizons are set based on the speed of change in the industry and the duration of investments—power plants last decades, as do bomber aircraft, laptops last for a few years, and fashion changes in weeks.
2. Baseline of the Current State that establishes the gap to the Target State. Using the future state as a guideline helps to contain the scope of the baselining exercise, because we focus on using the target state metrics, balancing metrics, and risk parameters.
3. Roadmap for Value Improvement: a program or a set of projects to take the company (or department, team, etc.) from the baseline to the target state. These programs are usually large in scope (e.g., company-wide or department-wide).

Value Improvement Planning is the first stage in this modeling technique. In this stage we design a roadmap to get to the target state and build the value improvement model to support its funding. This is a planning exercise, and if the plan is approved it drives investments and actions aligned to the roadmap (Fig. 4.10).

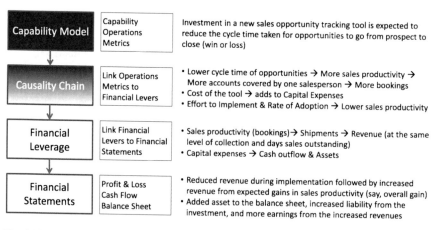

Fig. 4.10 Value improvement

---

[44] http://en.wikipedia.org/wiki/PDCA.

[45] http://en.wikipedia.org/wiki/Six_Sigma.

We take the results of Network and Capability modeling and use them to build a Value Improvement model that connects business and financial outcomes to the capability model. The connection uses two "bridging" mechanisms: first we tie the effects of the new (or changed) capability to a financial lever, and next we must connect the financial lever to the financial statements.

It is simple math to calculate financial leverage, such as the effect of reduction in "average days of sales outstanding" or "inventory turns" on the financial statements. The relationship of operational metrics to financial levers is less straightforward. We may expect sales productivity increases from a new system, but that productivity is lagged from the deployment and is also likely to be non-uniform (or maybe it does not materialize at all in some cases or for some companies).

We model causality chains using Influence Diagrams, that can handle propositions like the distribution of forecasts for project duration and cost, chances of project success (deployment of a new system) resulting in increases in employee productivity, etc. Due to the variability that we need to model, the model output generally includes a sensitivity analysis and we often present a set of selected scenarios (e.g., likely case, best case, worst case, etc.) or a spread of pathways to depict the variability in the forecast.

After the plan comes the decision to proceed. This may require us to make financial models for funding the plan—for example to lease or buy, to capitalize or expense, to fund internally or borrow, etc. The financial modelers may come back to the value improvement modelers with new constraints, such as to "self-fund" the program—i.e., to fund the program using the value created by its constituent steps. Decision makers may ask for changes—they may defer some projects, add new ones, make scope changes, etc. In such cases we need to rework the model.

Value Management: At checkpoints during the roadmap, we review the progress made in terms of project statuses and value realized. A data visualization model could use a timeline on the x axis, a value metric on the y axis, and a plot of the planned and actual states on the graph. We always find a deviation, nothing goes exactly to plan.

The idea is to understand what changed in the internal operations, in the environment and in the program itself. Assess the value realized to locate sources of value-capture or value-leakage.

The sources of value capture fall into two categories:

1. Expected sources of value are already in the model, and we test for actual capture against the plan, and look for root causes for over or under-capture
2. Unexpected sources of value may be found. A product may turn out to influence sales of related products, or gain penetration into unexpected market segments. We need to add these sources to the value model.

Value leakage also has two categories:

1. Going from project to results, we see leakages where the expected value contributions do not materialize. For instance, the adoption or penetration of new

behaviors has not happened as planned and that leads to lower-than-expected value realization—e.g., a new system for timecard entry is deployed but people keep using the old system, or resources can be assigned to projects online, but people continue to call up people to assign them to projects.

2. After we get the results, we encounter the reactions—competitors will see your results and launch counterattacks, employee unions may demand a greater share in profits, or suppliers may increase prices. Whenever you find a way to create new value or capture a larger share of it, there will be other parties who will try to figure out how to get some of it. This reaction, often from unexpected vectors, leaches away some of the expected value.

Next we update the model with our improved understanding of value leakages and value capture. In some cases we may need to create new sensors—new instruments to pick up data to defend against value leakages or to drive value capture.

Based on our new knowledge we may need to redesign the Network and Capability models, and adjust or revalidate the overall target state. Then we have to design and model an adjusted program to go from the new current state to the target state.

Checkpoints may be so closely spaced as to seem continuous. This is the dream of a truly adaptive control system, at the helm of which a management team steers the optimal course (Fig. 4.11).

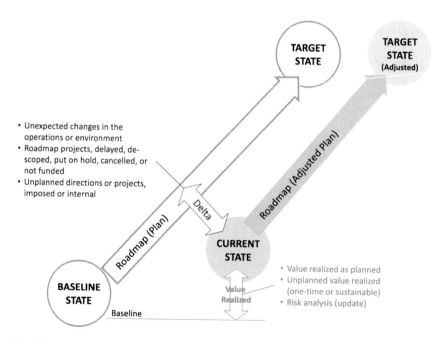

Fig. 4.11 Value management

Dashboards: to track their progress on an ongoing basis, most companies invest in making and using dashboards that show key performance indicators,[46] strategic scorecards or balanced scorecards[47] that present a view of the current state and its history, sometimes with updated forecasts. These dashboards are updated on scheduled cycles—quarterly, monthly, weekly, daily, etc.

The design of dashboards is rooted in the value improvement model, but represents a simplification so that people can see a "few key metrics" against which to set targets and track performance. The perspective changes—in this usage, the value improvement model is accessed by people who need to use the dashboard to assess their progress and to figure out if they need course-correction. To design dashboards, the considerations are:

1. Select metrics that represent the key goals of the business, with the right accuracy and sensitivity. Where there are multi-criteria goals, e.g., a goal to increase market share while maintaining margins, it must be represented by a metric for each criterion. Ensure that the selected metrics can be reliably calculated, so that people can learn to trust the dashboard.
2. Present the metrics in ways that people understand. Think about the medium for the dashboard and how people will use it so that you can design it as an effective tool for communication. Use recognizable or easily-learned patterns to help people navigate, such as

    a. Potential versus Target versus Actual (e.g., what is the Total Addressable Market size and growth, and where are we placed in it versus key competitors)
    b. Balanced Scorecards and Strategy Maps
    c. Journey maps that trace the transformation roadmap and place the current state in the context of the transformation. This metaphor may use qualitative elements such as "journey milestones" that recognize progress and celebrate incidents of successes aligned to the roadmap.

3. Provide context: compare the metric to the past, to key competitors, or to the target. Help people understand and internalize the messages the metrics convey.

Control views are used to watch for all the plethora of metrics that are used in the value model. Each metric can spawn many additional metrics needed to ensure reliability and accuracy which generates a set of data-quality metrics (e.g., a project margin metric requires that all project costs, dates, and revenues are accurately tracked)—these are children of the control metric. To manage the multiplicity of control metrics and their children, we often automate their monitoring by setting thresholds (control limits) and alerts.

Continuous Value Management: few companies have put in a control system that can continuously update the entire value improvement model. To run such a

---

[46] http://en.wikipedia.org/wiki/Key_performance_indicators.

[47] http://en.wikipedia.org/wiki/Balanced_Scorecard.

control system continuously (i.e., in near-real-time) requires data sources to be refreshed quickly, for the value models to be re-run rapidly, and for courses of action to be modeled as a simulation or a multi-user game. All these factors are increasingly within the reach of innovative leaders.

The financial markets rapid reaction to adjust prices based news, embodied in the efficient market hypothesis,[48] shows that it is possible to combine different value models on a large scale to drive rapid and largely accurate reaction. This case also illustrates that after you handle everything that a model can handle you are left with noise, exemplified by the "random walk"[49] of stock prices. It is this noise that requires any value improvement control system to be adaptive—robust against unexpected events, internal or external, large or small.

As we pursue increased automation of control systems we need to be aware of this surprising concern: the people who work with sophisticated real-time control systems, such as airplane pilots or ship's navigators, learn to trust them and forget how to react when the system encounters unexpected conditions—sometimes with catastrophic results.[50] The solution proposed by Parasuraman[51] is to design-in unreliability into the control system.

Optimization Systems Modeling

In certain cases we find the opportunity to use optimization models, for example to schedule trucks in a supply chain or work-orders in a factory, to allocate marketing spend, or to plan inventory, etc.

Optimization models embed optimization expertise as algorithms in data-driven systems that can be used by a broader set of people to drive from idea to execution. Expertise is applied to maintain or improve the system and its algorithms. In this way the expertise of a few people scales via the Optimization System to deliver a greater impact.

Let's model an example of scheduling work orders: we take requests (work order requests) and assign skilled services staff to work on them. The staff performs the assigned work and provides feedback with the project closure and time-cards.

The context diagram includes the other capabilities and models that supply inputs and create the feedback (learning) loop for the optimization model (Fig. 4.12)

---

[48] http://en.wikipedia.org/wiki/Efficient_market_hypothesis.

[49] http://en.wikipedia.org/wiki/Random_walk.

[50] http://spectrum.ieee.org/computing/software/automated-to-death.

[51] Parasuraman R, Molloy R, Indramani L (1993) Singh performance consequences of automation-induced complacency. Int J Aviat Psychol 3(1):pp 1–23.

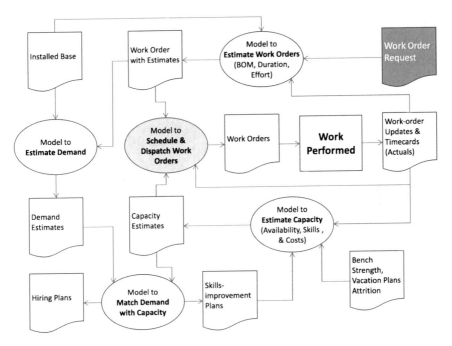

Fig. 4.12 Optimization systems model

The data visualizations will need to include not just the work order throughput and cycle time but also the accuracy and learning-curves of the estimations (work order estimates as well as overall capacity and demand), plan for demand/supply match, and the scheduling itself. The scheduling capability will need to assess the time it takes for scheduling and the effects of downstream adjustments to the schedule reflected in the actual timecards and work-order statuses—in this way it can learn and get better at its function.

Workflow Modeling

In the workflow layer the organization executes its work—we assign tasks to people or machines, provide the processes and procedures to do the work, and set up events and alerts to monitor the workflow.

Instrumenting and acting in this layer brings us into the world of "real time" analytics. To avoid getting caught up into what it means to be "real time" we prefer to name it inline analytics that operate within the timing requirements required by the business process, as opposed to offline analytics that cannot execute in line with the workflow but get used in the other offline layers (schedule, capacity, and strategy).

Decision modeling at the workflow layer is constrained to act within the context of a work assignment and its demands for timely execution. We can apply analytics models to make the workflows smarter. Execution layer analytics is also called Operational Intelligence.[52]

1. **Process** execution is done by trained people using Online Transaction Processing Systems (OLTP)[53] in alignment with policies and procedures (e.g., by the checkout agent at a grocery store to correctly generate the bill, to manage the coupons, make the cash and credit card transactions, and to ask customers if they found everything they needed).
2. **Assignment and dispatch** decisions are made by controllers or systems (e.g., to take the decision to assign another checkout agent); and
3. **Events and alerts** are used to trigger the process and to monitor execution (e.g., we can set an alert to watch for excessively long queues in the checkout lines)

Workflow modeling requires us to consider:

- Experience and training required for the people in the process
- System features that support analytics in-line with the process
- Policies and procedures to be followed
- Physical constraints of buildings, machine performance, etc.

Modeling Processes and Procedures

The context diagram to model processes and procedures looks like a flowchart.[54] We can instrument the process model to provide near-real-time visibility into the state of the processes. Such visibility to queues, bottlenecks, quality flags, yield/waste and throughput helps the capability managers react faster and more accurately to operational issues. It also provides data to upstream and downstream capabilities that enables them to coordinate better, to leverage transient opportunities, and to avoid small problems from rippling out to become bigger problems. In conjunction with an effective quality management process it can also be used to track quality more closely by continuously processing data about the quality of supplies (inputs), work centers, and deliverables. We can also use analytics on the processes to trigger exception process-branches or alerts.

In many cases, the flowchart diagram is not detailed enough and comes paired with a procedures document, and both are used to guide people on how work should be done. These procedure manuals can become large, and manifest as thick binders. Large manuals also lead to more demand for training and less compliance at the time of execution—people forget or make mistakes.

---

[52] http://en.wikipedia.org/wiki/Operational_intelligence.

[53] Online Transaction Processing Systems (OLTP) are a class of systems that manage Transaction oriented applications. We will discuss more on OLTP in the Business Intelligence chapter later in the book.

[54] http://en.wikipedia.org/wiki/Flowchart.

We can model "intelligent assistants" that can work in the context of work execution. They can offload some routine tasks, like the tasks executed by the first level of call center agents. They can monitor data streams in real time to detect problems, such if a caller is angry, and act on the information by triggering alerts. They can also provide context-sensitive help (appearing as a panel on a screen or a voice in your ear).

Modeling Assignment and Dispatch

When we encounter a decision box in a process, we should assess if an analytics model can select the exit path. For example, in a process to select insurance claims for detailed review as opposed to automatic approval, we could use analytics to determine which ones to select. This selection can be as basic as applying a one-parameter filter (look at the size of the claim—small ones are to get approved automatically, the rest to get reviewed), or as complex as consuming the results of an Expertise model that assesses the history of claims and picks out candidates for review based on calculations on a set of parameters.

The data visualizations track accuracy, false positives and false negatives, consistency, and learning. Sometimes a human operator is asked to review the machine recommendation, and in this case the data visualization and analysis needs to address the additional layer of decision-making.

Sophisticated assignment models can make a huge business impact. For example, routing calls accurately in a call center can reduce call duration and improve productivity.[55]

Even after an assignment is made to a work-center, the operator may be free to make further assignment decisions:

1. Before working on it, the work may be refused, escalated to a more skilled center, or switched to a different type of work-center as being misaligned to the nature of the assigned work-center. For instance, in a call center, a phone call may be routed to an agent who decides to take a break just then and refuses the call.
2. While working on it, the operator may encounter a situation where he needs to pass the work on to someone else. In a call center it may be that the caller demands to speak with the supervisor. In a service work-order it could be that the job turns out to be more complex than estimated and more help is needed.
3. After working on it, the assigned person may request a review or rework.

Because of the fact that these requests are exceptions in a process, they can be handled by looping them back into the queue, possibly with a pre-set priority (Fig. 4.13).

---

[55] http://www.fastcompany.com/36975/marketing-revolution.

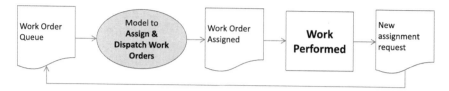

Fig. 4.13 Assignment model

The data visualization needs to reflect the incidence of these re-assignments. We look at first-pass yield to track accurate assignments and then zoom into analysis of the various categorize of re-assignments. This loop is used to help improve the performance of the Assignment and Dispatch model.

Modeling Events and Alerts

We need to model events when they carry business significance. A stock ticker is a set of events, as is a "heartbeat" signal from a deep-sea submersible or a Twitter posting. The first layer of modeling assesses the significance of the event itself (the stock moved 1 % down, or the Twitter feed reports a shooter on the campus). The second layer assesses the event in the context of other events, to locate patterns or correlated events. It can use this information to generate a new event that is the result of the pattern analysis. Such cascading analysis may be modeled with neural nets, and the industry term for the domain is "Complex Event Processing." It is used in algorithmic stock trading, security monitoring, network monitoring, etc.

Alerts are a class of events that are generated by the decision model when it determines that an alert is needed. To communicate or distribute an alert effectively, we also need to model the recipients, the channel to use, and the recipients' preferences for which alerts on which channels on which devices during what time-of-day, handling out-of-office and call-forwarding settings, acknowledgements, escalations, etc. Sometimes an alert message can come with a script for suggested responses to help guide the reaction. Immediate reactions, in turn, can be modeled as alerts, dispatch (assignment), or triggering a workflow.

Transparency, Integrity, Validity and Security

To ensure that decision models are not misused, they need to be transparent and verifiable. This is to assure the business that the model will do what we expect it to do. We need to protect against modeling mistakes by modelers, as well as from malicious intent.

Integrity of the model needs to be assured by methods that confirm that the verified model is the one in service.

To validate any one model or a set of related models, we use quality control processes that test if the model design conforms to the decision needs, that the deployed model conforms to the design, and that the results align to the decision need.

To validate the effects of all the models in use, sample how people experience your organization. Observe how the models work for people (employees, customers, suppliers, investors, etc.)—what do they experience? Review the throughput, delays, first-pass quality, variability, etc. Does it align to your strategy? If it does, you have tied together all the four layers of Ecosystem, Capability, Control Systems, and Workflows. If not, update your models.

To assure ongoing validity, establish ongoing or event-driven reviews of the decision models. This review process must draw from the internal data on how ideas flow to execution and also factor in external information about the industry, technology advances, regulatory environment, etc. In addition to the reviews, set up alarms to go off when key assumptions change—for instance, to warn when the confidence-ranges in the forecasting models have increased significantly, a node in the value network faces labor unrest, a new competitor enters the market, or that the housing mortgage market is threatened by a small and increasing trend for sub-prime loan default, etc.

Security of the model is another concern. If the model is subjected to attack and compromised, then we need to take it out of service to prevent its misuse from impacting business. The resulting degradation in service-levels caused by taking down the analytics models can itself impact business.

Deliverables from Decision Modeling

The result of a decision modeling cycle is an "analysis"—this can be as simple as a terse message, an Excel report, or a thick file that you take hours to read. In all their forms, the deliverables implicitly or explicitly embody the decision frame, the process of decision modeling (analysis), and the results of the analysis: findings, criteria, scenarios, options, and recommendations (Fig. 4.14).

- **Single criteria decision models** provide a set of choices that all achieve the same level of satisfaction for the criterion (strike-out the options that are lower).

	Criterion A
Option 1	202
Option 2	202
~~Option 3~~	~~201~~
Base case	111

In such analyses, double-check whether all the options are assessed and also the accuracy of the model. It is generally good practice to include a "base case" that depicts the outcome if the decision is not made. This enables the decision makers to assess the benefit of making the decision, as opposed to postponing it.

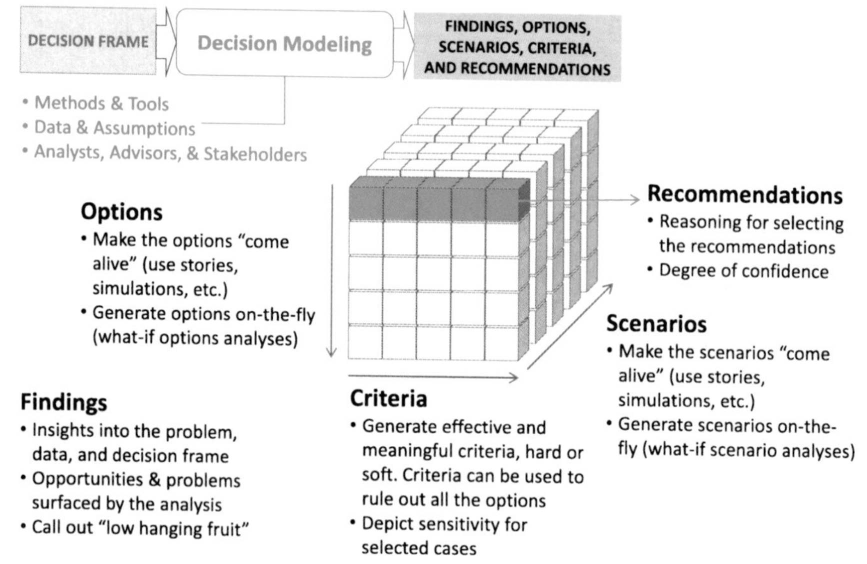

Fig. 4.14 Decision model deliverables

- **Multi criteria decision models** are generally used—we often put in the criteria of do-ability (our ability to do what it takes), value (in terms of costs, benefits, NPV, etc.), and risk. Present the decision matrix as a set of choices that are "Pareto Optimal" which means that you strike-out the options that are not as good as the selected ones, and you need to make trade-off decisions to select from the Pareto Optimal set. A trade-off curve (also known as an efficient frontier) is used to visualize the trade-off between two criteria.

	Criterion A	Criterion B	Criterion C
Option 1	89	50	56
Option 2	75	40	88
Option 3	100	30	50
~~Option 4~~	~~99~~	~~29~~	~~50~~
~~Option 5~~	~~70~~	~~40~~	~~88~~
Base case	43	23	12

Not only will you need to double-check whether all the options are assessed and the accuracy of the model—you'll also need to think about whether you have picked all the relevant criteria.

These analyses hold true for a context, or "scenario", that is the set of assumptions or forecasts. A high-growth scenario, for instance, can lead to a different option than a low-growth scenario. Scenarios can be modeled as sets of results. The performance of a decision-option across scenarios tests for how robust the option is against changes in context.

In cases where the analyses found "low hanging fruit"—opportunities such as excess inventory, excessive discounts, etc. that can be immediately converted by management directive—we can skip the step of creatively exploring options because it will not add value.

Decision modeling ends with the creation of an analysis that includes the model and its results: the statements of findings and recommendations. A checklist of steps that make up a good decision model includes:

- Establish the decision frame and objectives. This is used to keep everyone aligned.
- Provide data (or "evidence") that is factual and relevant. Findings establish useful facts, clearly identify opportunities, or remove misconceptions. In most cases we just present one selected model (hypothesis) but if you tested your model by trying to disprove it then you should provide evidence of this.
- Describe the criteria used to judge the options. Show that the decision criteria enable the selection of optimal choices.
- Present the range of feasible options (or "alternatives"), including the base case (i.e., the current course). Evaluate the performance of each option against the decision criteria.
- Make recommendations and compare to the base case. Link the recommended options to the opportunities addressed, and reiterate the expected results of selecting the recommended options.
- Suggest how to make the decision and outline actions required for decision execution.
- Provide a description of the analytical process, which is used to drive transparency and credibility—it provides a mechanism for constructive criticism and it builds credibility by enabling methodology and quality concerns to be addressed.

Chapter 5
Decision Making

The essence of management is making decisions. Managers are constantly required to evaluate alternatives and make decisions regarding a wide range of matters. Just as there are different managerial styles, there are different decision-making styles. Decision making involves uncertainty and risk, and decision makers have varying degrees of risk aversion. The role of the Decision modeling team is to present recommendations from the decision model in such a way that the decision maker can make a rational choice between the various alternatives presented.

The area of effective decision making is well researched and various business and academic luminaries have weighed in on the matter. People like Peter F. Drucker, Kathleen Eisenhardt, Ralph Keeney, John Hammond and several others have identified several key components of effective decision making. Some of these components focus on the individual decision maker, and some focus on the team dynamics where the decision maker plays in the organization.

In the current context, we will concern ourselves with behavioral and team attributes that lend themselves to effective data driven decision making. To enable successful executions of data driven decision making we need to focus on four critical areas.

Pose the right problem: Decision making will be ineffective if people do not understand the problem that needs to be addressed. Posing the right problem involves introspection and answers to questions like "What needs to be done?" and "Is this what I need to decide on?" Incorrect, Incomplete or Improper problem statement short change the decision maker and misguide the modeler and analyst in terms of what is expected of them. We looked at approaches to this area in the chapter on Decision Framing earlier in this book.

Understand the context: The context of the decision is the entire ecosystem that the decision need and the decision makers exist in. We have to consider the uncertainties, alternatives, risk and payoff (organizational and individual). This understanding helps us to eliminate bias and irrationality in the decision making process.

R. Saxena and A. Srinivasan, *Business Analytics*, International Series in Operations
Research & Management Science 186, DOI: 10.1007/978-1-4614-6080-0_5,
© Springer Science+Business Media New York 2013

Engage and debate: Many decision makers tend to avoid conflict, fearing it will bog down the decision-making process and degenerate into personal attacks. However, in a dynamic environment, conflict is a natural feature where reasonable managers will often diverge in assessments of how a market will develop. Conflict stimulates innovative thinking, creates a fuller understanding of options, and improves decision effectiveness. Without conflict, decision makers often overlook key elements of a decision and miss opportunities to question assumptions.

Eliminate irrationality and political considerations: Irrationality creeps into decision making in various forms and we need to be aware and cognizant of such irrationalities, actively eliminate them when they a rise and drive a culture of rational decision making. Politicking can be avoided by emphasizing a collaborative, rather than competitive, environment, and by creating common goals. Rather than implying homogeneous thinking, common goals suggest that managers have a shared vision of where they want to be.

The Role of the Decision Modeler

Decision makers are often experienced, and experience has taught them that business issues often recur after they have been attacked and even suppressed earlier. They want to take a systematic approach but struggle with the enormity of the challenge. They will welcome the help of analytics if they recognize that the analyst understands their world and are equipped to help. It is more difficult to translate this welcome into collaboration—to have the business executive work on decision modeling problems with analysts, where they're used to working with their peers and direct team while the analysts were "outside the room".

That presents a significant challenge to the decision modeler or the analyst. If analysts don't help the decision makers understand the model and to leverage the findings, then who will? The analyst will need to carry the analytics knowledge to the decision-making team—and the terrain for this expedition includes the inherent complexity of the decision domain, model limitations, decision-making biases, business volatility, and political cross-currents. Analysts can add significant value to the decision maker by making available the vast knowledge base in the analytics domain and drawing parallels and highlighting alternatives, risks, options that the decision maker may overlook.

Structure the decision making process as a process of inquiry in which the decision makers can participate effectively (Fig. 5.1).[1]

---

[1] Garvin DA, Roberto MA (2001) What you don't know about making decisions. Harv Bus Rev 79:108–116.

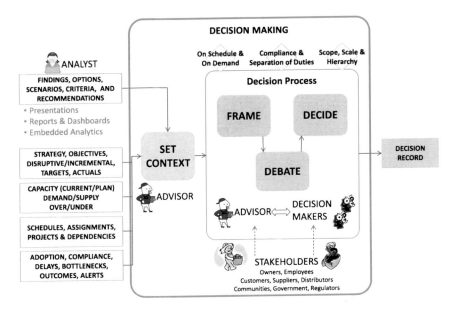

Fig. 5.1 Decision making

The Decision Making Method

The Decision Making Method has two phases: first where the decision model is placed into the business context (the "big picture" model of the business system), and second where the decision model is used for decision making. It presumes there is ongoing interlock with the decision-makers so that there is pre-existing familiarity with the decision models.

If key events in the decision process are put into a Decision Record, it will create the institutional memory needed for the organization to learn to become better at making decisions.

> When important decisions are not documented, one becomes dependent on individual memory, which is quickly lost as people leave or move to other jobs. In my work, it is important to be able to go back a number of years to determine the facts that were considered in arriving at a decision. This makes it easier to resolve new problems by putting them into proper perspective. It also minimizes the risk of repeating past mistakes. Moreover if important communications and actions are not documented clearly, one can never be sure they were understood or even executed.
> —Admiral Hyman G. Rickover, in a speech at Columbia University (1982)[2]

This "Decision Record" concept shows up as minutes of meetings, gets dissolved in the content of email archives, or in project management archives. We have not seen these records harvested for any use other than to shield managers

---

[2] http://govleaders.org/rickover.htm

against complaints or to provide backup material for blackening performance appraisals. As the domain and the decision coach role mature, we hope to see these decision records being used to create a learning loop to improve decision making.

Set Context

In this stage, take the decision model deliverables (findings, options, recommendations, etc.) and integrate them with the existing business context. The context elements are the sum of the ecosystem, capabilities, control systems and workflow views—put together they represent the business vision, strategy, and current state (Fig. 5.2).

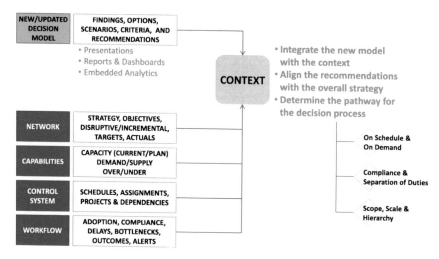

Fig. 5.2 Decision context

Integrate the new or updated decision model with the context. Assess and communicate how the integration changed the context—decision makers will need to understand the change, and the analysts need to know this too. Review the model results in this new context, and assess how they align with strategy (or adjusted strategy). Communicate the new context and alignment back to the analyst teams and forward to the decision process. This context-setting requires the analyst to:

1. Balance disruption against drift—set a "damping level" to tune the organization responsiveness (neither over-damped and delayed nor under-damped and swinging wildly)
2. Retest for the organization's capacity to absorb the decision—can this be added on to the existing workflows? Does the model include the trade-offs on prioritizing what can be dropped?

3. Think through what the decision would mean for stakeholders:

    a. What change is needed, and how will it be cascaded into communications, goal-setting, and performance reviews? Will employees see it as aligned with their current goals and incentives?
    b. What is the impact on customers, the distribution chain and supply chain, and competitors?
    c. What is the impact on the brand and on communities? On regulators' viewpoints?

4. Check how the model handles dependencies and aligns with other decisions in the pipeline and with the overall organization direction (e.g., a small proposal may be dropped in favor of a larger transformation that the modelers may not know of).

In cases where the integration creates a significant change, it forks the context from the previous state. Now you need to maintain both states because the decision process may choose to reject the new model and stay with the old one. These fork events become part of the context.

Depending on the kind of decision to be made, the decision pathway is to be selected. Review the decision to be made: is it part of the routine (falls within the pre-existing decision context) or does it change the context? Assess the urgency, importance, scale and scope of the decision. Based on these factors, we select an appropriate path for the decision process, which could be:

On Schedule and On Demand—we can introduce the decision need in a scheduled governance meeting, or request a special meeting.

Compliance and Separation of Duties—we need to ensure that we account for checks and balances in decision making based on the duties of the decision makers. Separation of duties assures cross-checking of a decision within the pathway. Compliance is used to ensure that the company policies are followed in the pathway for the decision.

Scope, Scale and Hierarchy—based on the scale and scope of the decision we need to route the decision to the appropriate decision makers. In many cases, the decision makers can cascade the request to their staff, or delegate their authority. This becomes path of the decision pathway.

Decision Process

The decision process needs to be a process of inquiry, understanding, debate, agreement, and commitment. This is in contrast with the process of advocacy, in which we push our model and recommendations. The role of the decision makers is to make informed and rational decisions. We need to help them do so. In trivial cases the decision is clear and maybe the only reason it came into the process was for reasons of compliance. We'll not spend time in that case, and focus on the non-trivial case where a decision of consequence needs to be taken. The process for this is Frame, Debate, and Decide.

Step 1: Frame

For important decisions, start with framing the context of the decision. Explain the current state, and describe the decision model that is in use. Present the findings (facts and issues, items that help people understand what is at stake in the discussion), discuss the assumptions and criteria that the analysts have used in the model, and step through the scenarios and options. In cases where the Decision Modelers' recommendations will not stifle debate, present the recommendations too.

In this stage, ensure that people are able to place the decision in the business perspective that includes assessment of feasibility, immediate and long-term effects of the available courses of action, alignment with strategic direction, and external business trends. In some cases it also helps to tell the story of how the decision was framed and modeled, and who was involved in those activities.

Step 2: Debate

For important decisions, test for the existence of conflict. Are there two or more divergent opinions? If not, we are in danger of groupthink[3] or falling into our comfort zone. In this phase, we need to:

- Stimulate debates. If there is no natural owner in the decision-making group of a dissenting position, appoint one. Help change perspectives of participants by having them take on roles of stakeholders that are different from the ones they usually represent. List and question assumptions, air doubts, bring objections to the table. Create sub-groups who can discuss the issue and develop differing viewpoints that inject variety into the debate.
- Get external experts into the process, and have these experts available to the decision makers. These "outsiders" are not core members of the decision making group and should be empowered to challenge the decision makers.
- Help people frame their interests as criteria, make trade-offs, identify give-and-take required within the decision making team, help facilitate the negotiations, and where possible to arrive at win–win situations.

Step 3: Decide

At the appropriate time a decision is required—not too early so that it cuts out productive debate, and not so late that positions harden or the delay propagates

---

[3] http://en.wikipedia.org/wiki/Groupthink

the status quo. As we assess for when to precipitate the decision, we need to see if the group is getting polarized[4] or if the team has not yet surfaced their preferences.[5]

To execute the decision step, leverage the research on the factors that lead to improved decisions:

- Review the decision model. Annotate it with the highlights from the debates. If it evolved during the debate, show how it evolved.
- Re-evaluate the findings, assumptions, criteria, scenarios, options and recommendations. Help the team remember the debates about the alternatives (options), calibrate the facts, and list the assumptions.
- If you think the team has almost arrived at a decision but may not have fully thought it through, use the "premortem" technique[6] to help them think through the course of action.
- Revisit the decision criteria to avoid situations where people compromise on criteria because they want to close a deal.
- Engage the team to make the decision using a fair and transparent procedure.
- To confirm the decision, we can either ask a "Devil's advocate" to criticize the decision or take an anonymous poll of the group. If we find people want to change the decision, loop back to the start of this step.

Decision Making Roles

From the discussion on the decision making process, we can derive the need for these two Decision Making Roles:

1. Decision makers, who make the decisions, and
2. Advisors are "decision coaches" who guide and facilitate the decision making process.

Decision makers carry the responsibility to familiarize themselves with the business context and decision model, and work with the decision process to arrive at the best decisions for the business. In many cases, decision makers work closely with modelers to frame and flesh out the model, and downstream to drive the implementation and results.

Advisors are needed to drive the Decision Making Method—to work with analysts and with the decision makers to help the business navigate through the shoals of decision-making errors and to both arrive at the best possible decision and also

---

[4] http://en.wikipedia.org/wiki/Group_polarization

[5] http://en.wikipedia.org/wiki/Abilene_paradox

[6] A technique by which failure of a decision (or project) is assumed (in the initial stages) and people analyze the reasons for the failure. Klein G (2007) Performing a project premortem. Harv Bus Rev 85:18–19.

experience a decision process that is transparent, fair, and rational. The positive process attributes are needed so that decision makers feel satisfied with the decision they made and commit to its success.

Stakeholders (e.g., employees, suppliers, distributors, customers, etc.) are represented in the process by proxy—by the analyst, advisor, and decision makers. At all stages, be able to take a stakeholder viewpoint and assess their costs, benefits, risks and perceptions. To do this effectively, you have to be in ongoing contact with stakeholders. Such contact must be at first-hand for the advisors.

Biases, Emotions, and Bounded Rationality

The problem with rational decision making is that humans rely on their emotions to take decisions and often shy away from complexity. The state of "analysis paralysis" is real—people get stuck with thinking about the complexity of the decision, and don't take the decision. After an analysis is conducted and presented by a leader, the decision-making process kicks in, and this process is often rife with politics.

Emotion is not the enemy—there is research to show that when brain damage removes your ability to feel emotion you also become indecisive (such as the case of Elliot as described in the book "How We Decide" by Jonah Lehrer).

When you can avoid analysis paralysis, you can run into a shoal of decision biases.[7] These biases come in many forms, such as:

- **Overconfidence**: People generally and consistently overestimate their ability to make the right decision or remember facts accurately. They may not realize that their decisions are less-than-optimal, so they will not see the need to use data driven analyses.
- **Emotion Risk**: Emotions change our risk perception. Anger and happiness both reduce the risk we perceive, so we make riskier decisions in these emotional states. Fear makes us risk averse, and to avoid making decisions.
- **Loss Aversion**: Loss aversion is our bias towards avoiding a loss as opposed to making a gain. This bias can be exploited during the decision-making process— just by framing alternatives with words such as "lose" or "gain" we can change people's perception of the model.
- **Confirmation Bias**: We select and remember information that supports our bias, even if the data is not reliable, and forget or discount other information.

---

[7] Hammond JS, Keeney RL, Raiffa H (2006) Hidden traps in decision making. Harv Bus Rev 76:47–48.

- **Indecision or Avoidance**:This stems from various factors such as lack of effective dialog[8] or from just getting overwhelmed by choice (more choices lead to fewer decisions).[9]
- **Counter Intuitive Recommendations**: Reliance on "gut feelings" or rules (heuristics) that can lead us astray, for example thinking that something is dangerous because you have read about it, leading you to mistakenly believe untruths such as that nuclear power generation has caused more deaths than power from burning coal. This is very commonly observed when the decision model offers recommendations that are "counter-intuitive" to our experiences. It is very easy to discount and disregard the model as being "wrong", but this also presents the most impactful opportunities for analytics. Such scenarios are the perfect examples where intuition-based decision making would have been inferior to data driven analytical decision making.

In addition to biases, we face our human limitations, our bounded rationality:

1. We are expected to fully understand the ramifications and intelligently discount pursuing details that will not add value, but how do we know for sure if we have framed and scoped the analysis correctly? How can we assure ourselves that we have considered all feasible options?
2. We are expected to select the best analytical techniques for the situation and to use it correctly. Can we claim to have the full understanding of all analytical techniques needed to do so? Can we correctly specify, test, and correct a complex analysis that uses advanced mathematical techniques?
3. We need to have fixed decision criteria with fixed weights for selecting the best option. Can we weight and stick to our decision as needed for this? Do we want to change the weights or add criteria to "play" with its effect on the recommended option?

Knowingly or unknowingly, we can also introduce misrepresentations in the data. Can we resist doctoring the analyses and presentations to paint us in a better light or to lead the team to the decision we desire? Are we always diligent about data quality, confidence levels, and assumptions about the data distributions (is it always a normal distribution)? Do we always present the graph axis starting at zero or sometimes "zoom in" for effect? Have you ever felt that the request to revisit the analysis came from recommending an option that the leader did not want?

These are other subtle factors that bring inbuilt biases and limitations to the fore. Used correctly, these can be powerful factors in influencing decision making.

Priming, Anchoring, and Availability effects bias you without triggering awareness that you may be biased:

- Making people think of money makes them more independent and selfish—just pictures of money on a computer screen saver is enough to change the behavior of people.

---

[8] Charan R (2006) Conquering a culture of indecision. Harv Bus Rev 84:108–117.

[9] Iyengar SS, Lepper MR (2000) When choice is demotivating: can one desire too much of a good thing? J Pers Soc Psychol 79: 995–1006.

- The listing price of a house affects your judgment of how much it is worth. A similar effect is seen with some goods like Wine, where price is seen as an indicator of quality.
- People become less confident about a choice if they are asked to list twelve arguments to support their choice rather than six. Students who were asked to list more ways to improve a course rated it higher.

Truth Illusions reduce the strain of understanding, and predispose us to accept the message:

- Stories are compelling, and the ones that are easier to remember rest on few facts, while reality is complex and never neatly ordered.
- Text printed in bright blue or red is more likely to be believed than text in shades of green, yellow, or pale blue.
- High quality paper, high-contrast fonts and prints.
- Simple sentences, easily-pronounced names (easy to remember, familiar).

Visual Illusions lead to impressions that do not correspond to the underlying data:

- Charts with axes that do not start at zero, skip intervals, change scales, represent 2D data in 3D, represent time-series as categories, etc. are used to magnify or reduce the effects of the facts represented by the data.
- Data-points that skip over intermediate periods can sometimes be useful to deal with seasonality but are generally suspect.

Statistical Illusions are patterns in randomness that look like "stories" or cause-effect chains:

- Regression to the mean explains why bad performances are generally followed by improved performance and great performances are followed by a declines.
- Sampling effects—disease clusters and health clusters show up in small communities as a function of random distribution, but our focus shifts to explaining the "root causes" for the cluster.

Managing Irrationality: Removing Bias from Analytics

There is a lot of literature on avoiding decision-making pitfalls[10] and to use "evidence-based management".[11] Here are a few methods that can mitigate the effects of the biases and limitations inherent in decision making:

1. **Establish a data driven decision culture**—enable a culture where decisions must be data driven and irrational decisions or postponements are questioned. Data-selection biases can be mitigated by driving diversity in the team.

---

[10] Kahneman D, Lovallo D, Sibony O (2011) The big idea: before you make that big decision. Harv Bus Rev 89:50–60.

[11] Pfeffer J, Sutton RI (2006) Evidence-based management. Harv Bus Rev 84:62–74.

A person with a different point of view can bring in data that the team may have unwittingly ignored. Assigning people to a questioning role, such as the "Devil's Advocate" role, also reduces the potential for mistakes by forcing cross-checks and surfacing new questions.

2. **Review the decision-models**—arrange for peer reviews, collaborate with people outside the organization who can bring in new thoughts and knowledge, and keep up with the developments in the domain. Question whether all feasible options were considered, all relevant criteria are addressed, and test to check if the model has errors. Check for corner-cases and edge-cases; use an arsenal of quality assurance techniques. Diversity of the team members and inclusiveness in team processes also correlate with increasing creativity, which is needed to explore and improve the model and to reduce the effects of groupthink and bounded rationality.

3. **Enforce presentation guidelines**—set and follow rules for presentation of data and description of options that reduce the opportunity for misrepresentation and promote critical thinking. Training on inclusive behaviors enables analysts to build presentation content and formats that enable the decision makers to participate effectively in the decision process.

4. **Decision-making guidelines**—set and follow rules that promote open discussion, minimize the effects of authority, and leverage the group's diverse viewpoints. This step, however, proves paradoxically hard—the more complex the problem, the greater the reliance on experts who then become authority figures. Also, in many cases the set of decision makers is different from the set of analysts who built the decision model and the decision-support presentation. To help the decision-makers understand the analysis without blocking too much time in the decision-making forum agenda, decision makers should work with the analysts beforehand and evolve the model based on these discussions. In this process, the benefit is that the decision-makers move upstream into the decision analysis role and this improves the decision quality by reducing the gap between the analysts and the decision makers.

5. **Establish a learning-by-doing culture**—once a decision is made, put it in use right away and start to monitor the effects. This teaches the organization to act, and to learn what works and what does not. The objective data flow is needed to wash out the effects of subjective thinking and biases. The path of fast-acting and fast-correcting organizations may not look smooth and straight, but over time such adaptive behavior proves highly effective. This method is required to drive out irrationality over time, while the other methods act as sieves that help to direct decisions towards rationality.

It is hard work to make rational decisions. Do it when it is needed—when the analysis (advice) will convert to actions, and actions to results. If the analysis is window-dressing, do not waste your time on improving it. If your brother has already chosen the woman he will marry, your analysis of the match may not be valuable. If your analysis does not support a call to action (which includes a "stay the course" action), think again about why you produced it.

Chapter 6
Decision Execution

After deciding, we execute … or maybe not. Not all decisions are executed, or converted from a nominal "implementation" to behavioral changes and then business results. Advisory and assessment projects generally suffer from these defects. Transformation and experimentation engagements do close the loop from model to result with ongoing governance and assessments, but the actual work of driving the decision from record to results is often left outside the purview of analytics.

Often the biggest complaint by analytics teams is that the "business" does not execute on the decisions that they worked on. We assert that the role of the analytics teams requires them to support execution. It is a widespread practice to have the analytics teams design reports and build dashboards that are used to track and communicate execution. They simply need to step up to fully owning the Decision Execution function as defined in this chapter (Fig. 6.1).

To get and prove results from data driven decision making, we need to connect the decision modeling & decision making processes to decision execution, actions, and to subsequent data gathering and assessment to measure the results of the decisions. We need to work with the decision makers, often line-of-business managers, to act upon the decisions. We also need to get out of the comfort zone of making models. We should observe and influence the organization and its environment to make the decision play out to results.

Three decision execution activities are required to get from decisions to results:

1. Align & Enable
2. Observe & Report
3. Communicate & Converse

Align & Enable

The organization is generally already in motion, guided by plans and goals laid down in earlier cycles. It becomes our job to evolve the plans and goals to align with the new decisions. This may require us to wait for the next goal-setting cycle

R. Saxena and A. Srinivasan, *Business Analytics*, International Series in Operations
Research & Management Science 186, DOI: 10.1007/978-1-4614-6080-0_6,
© Springer Science+Business Media New York 2013

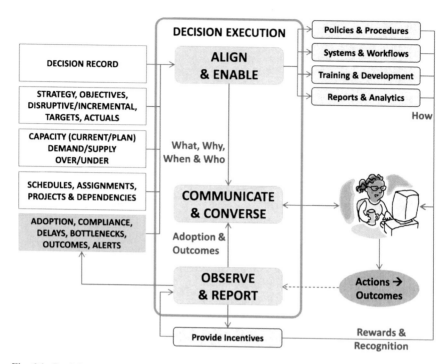

Fig. 6.1 Decision execution

or the next governance meeting (a yearly, quarterly, or monthly event) in which to embed the execution. Ensure that there is a clear value proposition to execute the decision and that there is a way to measure the value. To reduce the degree of expertise needed to execute the new workflows we enable changes in

1. **Processes & Procedures**: Assess how the decision impacts existing processes and procedures. Where needed, we need to work with the process owners to make the updates (adds, changes, or deletions), set the schedule for when the updates take effect, and get into the loop for communicating the changes so that we can track and enable its success.
2. **Systems & Workflows**: Automate and embed the new decisions into system workflows, features &reports so that more people can work smoothly within the desired process. The process can be arbitrarily complex, and can use outputs from sophisticated tools such as schedule optimization systems that use a complex mathematical model.
3. **Training & Development**: Where people will need training on the new processes, systems, and analytics, work with the training team to enable its delivery.
4. **Reports & Analytics**: In most cases the new decision needs new or updated reports to help the business see what to do differently and for managers to track the compliance, adoption, and possible bottlenecks or side-effects of the decision. We need to work with the report-making and analytics teams to

build the new analytics. Dashboards and reports are used on an ongoing basis to communicate and provide the analyses used to anchor the collaborative effort. Management dashboards and reports track actions and results (adoption, compliance, and value realized). Exception lists and alerts are used to reduce non-compliance, identify bottlenecks, and reward desired behaviors.

Observe & Report

In this activity we assess the actual actions and results against targets. Before cutover we track the execution project timelines for deployment projects, monitor the on-time and delayed cutovers. Program managers jockey the various threads to completion: changes to processes, systems, training, and analytics, across different places and different teams. After cutover we look for adoption of the decision—the signs of behavior changes that will drive value. And finally we look for the indicators of value, and estimate the value realized. At the same time we look for new bottlenecks (Did we just shift the bottleneck with our intervention? Do we see other queues form or lengthen?). We also investigate the root causes of non-adoption or partial adoption, so that we can adjust the execution.

Sometimes, as we observe increasing call-waiting times, frazzled sales reps managing customer defections or chasing missing shipments we find that we are in the middle of a failed project, one that should be rolled back or rescued. In this position, we can provide objective data about the situation that will be needed to fix the problems.

We may even be the early-warning system to find issues with decision execution before they snowball into crisis. This is especially true if you are closely monitoring the pre-cutover activities of training (look for feedback from the trainees after they complete the training) and systems test cycles (look at the open bugs and what they imply for the system functionality, volume/load tests for performance, etc.).

Since this team observes execution, it is also well-placed to help the organization to **Provide Incentives**. It is a manager's job to hand out rewards, recognize good behaviors and correct misaligned behaviors, and the managers are happy to get help to figure out where rewards are due and where corrective action is needed. We can use our observations to drive the analytics that align the organization's rewards and recognition mechanisms towards the updated goals, actions and results.

The real world of incentives and performance measurement is pretty complex, layered and nuanced. People respond to incentives, and in most companies the incentives for target-setting activities are to lie.[1] This particular distortion lives in the "Provide Incentives" box in the diagram, and infests non-linear pay-for-performance programs that arise in several places, from sales incentives to machine shops.[2] When your

---

[1] Jensen MC (2003) Paying people to lie: the truth about the budgeting process. Eur Finan Manag 9:379–406.

[2] Roy D (1952) Quota restriction and goldbricking in a machine shop. Am J Sociol 57(5):427–442.

project attempts to put analytics on these folks' behaviors to raise productivity or increase revenues from, you will learn the perverse effects of the incentives that can often wash out the naively well-intentioned effects of the decision you are driving.

As you make your observations in this context, think deeply about the root causes of what you see. You'll see sales spikes at period-ends, more customer-returned-goods just after the period, discounts that are all over the map, etc., and will need to conduct your analysis in the background noise of these transactions extract the signal of your decision execution project.

Communicate & Converse

We need to tell people about the decisions and the new behaviors expected, listen to feedback, and evolve the decision if needed. Feedback loops are needed to figure whether or not the decisions are leading to the desired outcomes. To change behavior, people generally need to understand both what (e.g., what to start, stop, or continue doing) and why it makes sense to change. We need to have a conversation with them to help them to understand the reasons for the change and then to change their behaviors.

This conversation occurs in the context of your target audience's needs and motivations. In general, we communicate messages about how our project is interesting, meaningful and relevant. These messages are sent in the context of the strategy and purpose of the team. There are, however, several other levers that can be used to drive behaviors and get results (Fig. 6.2).

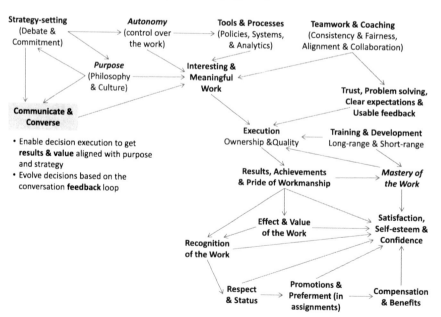

Fig. 6.2 Motivational context for decision execution

In the diagram, we can trace the motivational context of a business worker who seeks "purpose, mastery and autonomy"[3]—and as we trace it we find other elements that are useful for our communication. The effect and value of the work you do is an intrinsic motivator, and people feel better about their work when they meet and talk to people who gain the benefits of it. Other such levers can be used to place the execution in the overall context of the business network and strategy, so that people naturally adopt the changed behaviors and benefit from the results of the decision execution. A common piece of advice for communications is to think about "What's In It For Me" (WIIFM) from your audience's point of view, and a diagram like this will help you construct that viewpoint.

In general there will be other teams that manage communication—we position the analytics role in this function as being specialized towards scientific observation, analysis, and communication of complex and noisy data-sets. In this focused role, we would fill a glaring gap in the processes and staffing of decision execution teams. We can analyze the communications stream and assess if the communications mix can be improved—maybe it is too heavy on the adoption rate and missing out on the customer effect, etc.

---

[3] http://www.ted.com/talks/dan_pink_on_motivation.html

Chapter 7
Business Intelligence

Business Intelligence refers to a collection of tools and techniques for data management, analysis and decision support. It is the most commonly-referenced function of the Analytics Domain. In fact, in several cases, this component is mistaken to represent the entire Analytics Domain. As outlined in the Framework for Analytics, BI simply represents one component of a successful analytical framework. While it may be obvious that such a limited view of analytics usually dooms analytical aspirations, there are several reasons (historical, political, financial and serendipitous) why such a perception is endemic and it is critical to understand these reasons if one is to ensure success in an organization's analytical aspirations.

A Brief History of Data Infrastructure

Data remains the most critical ingredient of successful analytical capabilities and much emphasis has, justifiably, been placed on building infrastructure to collect data that can be used for analytics.

1990s: The evolution of data collection and infrastructure systems can be traced back to the early 1990's when ERP systems started gaining prominence. These ERP systems link corporate databases to support various business processes like Sales, HR, finance, Customer Service etc. While earlier systems and processes existed that served the same function, it was not until the 1990's that the function of data collection and infrastructure was called out as an independent focus area. This also coincided with the launch of PC (Personal Computer) reporting solutions like *Crystal Reports, Microstrategy EIS Toolkit, Qlik Technologies,* etc. These ERP systems typically called for huge investments from the corporates to ensure the IT infrastructure was scalable and capable of handling these ERP systems. The Y2K (Year 2000) phenomenon[1] served to accelerate

---

[1] http://en.wikipedia.org/wiki/Y2K

R. Saxena and A. Srinivasan, *Business Analytics*, International Series in Operations Research & Management Science 186, DOI: 10.1007/978-1-4614-6080-0_7,
© Springer Science+Business Media New York 2013

this ERP "migration" as companies scrambled to revamp IT systems to identify and eliminate the Y2K bug, ERP systems offered a "off the shelf" solution that improved the IT and Data infrastructure while also eliminating the Y2K challenges of legacy systems. Consequently, IT systems began to collect large volumes of data that were hitherto unheard of. Towards the end of the decade, the term "Business Intelligence" started making its way into the vocabulary, as IT organizations sought to find ways to capitalize an unexpected asset that was building up—data.

The rising growth of the Internet as a commercial platform, coupled with the ever reducing cost of storage, and growth of computational capabilities significantly accelerated the rate and scope of data collection.

Since the Y2K challenge and the ERP system upgrades were seen as a purely IT function, a lot of critical and foundational decisions were made on the data infrastructure by IT departments, with little or no vision of the end state of the consumption of data.

A slew of vendors started selling a variety of solutions that could collect, collate and query and retrieve large volumes of data very efficiently. These very loosely corralled under a category of "BI Vendors" and they invested in, and advanced the space in the frontier that was the need of the hour—efficiency in Data storage and retrieval.

The 2000s: As organizations began to come to terms with the richness and volume of data that was available, sophisticated analytical techniques for forecasting and predictive modeling began to become feasible. Specialized analysts with expertise in statistical and mathematical modeling were sought after as organizations started waking up to the possibilities of better decision making using data. Towards the end of the decade, specialized "analytics" teams begin to make their appearance in various forms and shapes.

The ecosystem started to see two very distinct phenomena.

- The growth of specialized vendors who provided services in the area of statistical and mathematical modeling.
- The logical extension of the BI Vendors rebranding as "Analytics Solution Providers" by leveraging their data infrastructure and add value added features and services on top.

As with any nascent industry (analytics was big enough to be called an "Industry" by now), the term "Analytics" was defined and redefined frequently and usually to suit the convenience of the people spending the most money. The large, successful BI vendors (now Analytics Solution Providers) set the standards and definitions of what was and what was not covered under the auspices of "Analytics". However, it was only to be expected that, given their roots in IT, these definitions leaned towards technology and systems and less with the business uses and needs of analytics.

When one looks at the state of the industry today armed with this very brief history lesson, some symptoms seen (up to) today become obvious.

- A large number BI projects fail—a recent Gartner study estimated that less than 30 % of BI projects were deemed to meet the needs of the Business.[2]
- Funding for analytics and BI initiatives will be less dependent on IT budgets, but rather on Business Units to drive the analytics that they need—it is estimated that by 2012, Business Units will control and contribute at least 40 % of the BI budget.[3]
- Companies that involve the Business Users in their BI initiative show more success that those who do not—*BI Scorecard 2011* Survey findings.

Business Intelligence for Analytics

The evolution of BI data infrastructure can be put into three stages:

1. **Single-Pass Analytics Systems**—this is the design-point for most current BI tools. This design imagines a situation where data flows linearly from OLTP to BI to the reports used by analysts. In this case, the data flow looks like it hits a "dead end" in the analyses ... and we jokingly say that analyses is where data goes to die. Wherever this stage is implemented, it quickly moves to the next stage.

2. **Overlapped Analytics Systems (Single-Pass and Looped)**—in the real world, analysts get data from various systems (not just the official BI databases) and process it in their own analyses that are provided to decision makers. They do this because business needs evolve and the demand for analyses cannot be met by the tools that were designed for a past state of affairs. This creates data loops, which manifest downstream in overlapping and conflicting reports. Battling against this stage by trying to revert to the previous stage proves unproductive—it is very expensive to generate the capacity to rapidly address ad hoc needs by adding them into the "production grade" BI data infrastructure, and impossible to engineer tools to meet all possible analytics needs in the future. Agility is required, and either exacts its toll of confusion and costs (in this stage) or enables the case for transition to the next stage that is designed for agility.

3. **Closed-Loop Analytics Systems** are the next generation in the BI evolution. This stage aligns the data-flows and data-stores in support of the analytics function, and avoids the loops and overlaps in the previous stage (Fig. 7.1).

---

[2] "Predicts 2012: Business Intelligence Still Subject to Nontechnical Challenges"—Gartner Research ID Number G00227192.

[3] Rick van der Lans, international BI expert from R20/Consultancy, ITWeb BI Summit, Feb 2012.

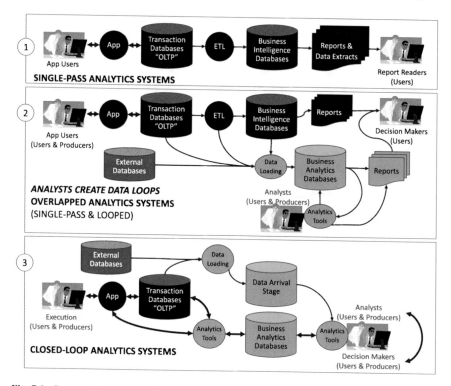

Fig. 7.1 Stages of business intelligence

There is a huge conflict in the second stage between analysts who continuously evolve their own models and their IT counterparts who encode models into the databases and data flows in the form of database designs (such as tables, views, and hierarchies), data transformations, stored procedures, dashboard designs, etc. In the third stage this conflict is resolved by separating the concept of input data (stored in a "Data Arrival Stage") and model data (stored in "Business Analytics Databases"). In this design you have high fidelity between the data sources and the Data Arrival Stage—i.e., there is no need to spend money to encode any data manipulations to the input data. Then analysts are empowered to use the input data to create the Business Analytics Databases that prove to be both robust and agile.

Business Intelligence in the Analytics Framework

Business Intelligence is one of the six parts of the Business Analytics Framework. The Business Intelligence function includes several assets (databases, systems, tools) and processes that interact with the other functions of the analytics framework. In this chapter, we will take a closer look inside the Business Intelligence function and understand the various assets and processes that belong to it. The various assets, processes and interaction with the rest of analytics framework are depicted below (Fig. 7.2).

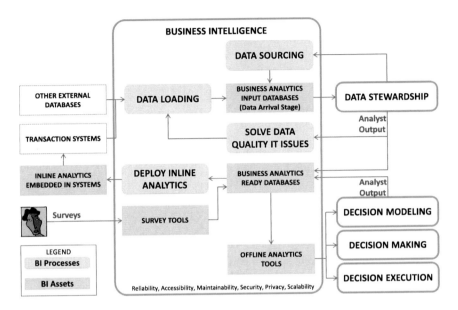

Fig. 7.2 Business intelligence

The BI function is responsible for providing the technology underpinning analytics. Measure success in this endeavor by benchmarking against peers and also against what is possible using today's technology. The actual use of analytics technology may be gated by business culture or the analytics teams' capabilities, and BI should not pull ahead to over-invest in analytics technology.

In any case it helps to assess where the BI technology stands against a scale of what's possible:

1. Unable to provide analytics systems (data, tools and infrastructure).
2. Partially provides the analytics systems and data required and refreshes the data periodically for off-line analyses.
3. Fully provides analytics systems and refreshes the data periodically for off-line analyses.
4. Enables analytics to be executed in-line, i.e., used seamlessly within business processes.
5. Delivers enterprise-wide in-line analytics, so the organization can use analytics at scale and without delay.

This information can be used to coordinate technology improvements in the overall analytics maturity framework that includes culture, capability, and technology.

Data Sourcing

Data Sourcing is needed to get input data for analytics, where the customer for the data is the data stewardship team. Data is sourced from a variety of systems each presenting its own unique challenges for a Business Intelligence system. This activity deals with the challenges of trying to get data from various sources as needed by analysts, and we will address four types of sources.

Transaction Processing Systems

Online Transaction Processing systems (OLTP) are a class of systems that facilitate and manage transaction oriented applications. These range from e-commerce sale transactions and credit card transactions to employee time-card applications. These systems are geared to handle large volumes of transactions efficiently and capture data for each transaction. This captured data is a primary source of data for BI systems and usually form the cornerstone around which effective data warehouses are built.

Given the need for accuracy and reliability of such systems, data from such sources also is of high fidelity. Transactions cannot be completed and logged with incomplete or inaccurate data (in most cases), and hence data sourced from such systems are among the most reliable. Data errors, if identified down the line, are often amenable to remedy by a suitable mechanism introduced in the OLTP (more on this under the topic of Data Quality later in this chapter).

Benchmarks and External Data Sources

While OLTP systems provide significant volumes of data, they tend to be myopic in that they only address the processes and systems that they support. More often than not, that does not provide a sufficient representation of data to support sophisticated analytical models. BI systems can source data sources external to the organization. Such data are typically provided by vendors who collect and collate data for the industry across organizations and provide such data for a fee. Examples include retail Point-of-Sale data from generic brand retail outlets; Industry data for Salary and Benefits comparison, social-media feeds from Twitter, Google Analytics, etc. Government and financial markets data sources are also available for download and use. Where surveys and benchmarking activities are outsourced to specialist providers, we count them as external data sources.

While the richness and the capabilities enabled by such data are beyond question, the quality and reliability of this data proves to be a significant deterrent to its widespread adoption.

For starters, aligning this data against internal hierarchies and dimensions is fraught with danger, since the process of collation necessarily obfuscates such organization specific data and instead uses some generic classification. For instance, the organizations may choose to view the US and Canada as two distinct sales regions, but the retail sales data may choose to tag them collectively under "North America". Such disconnects could make such data unusable for analytics, or limit the scope of analytical models.

In addition, such data sources are never exhaustive, in that, they never truly capture all the market activity. Channels that are too new or too small to be captured under this umbrella will be missed. Depending on how fragmented the market is, this could pose significant challenges for analytical modeling. For instance, Point-of-Sale retail data will miss out sales from small retailers, mom and pop stores, as well as direct e-commerce sales. Since various competitors/products have strengths in different channels, this could introduce a significant bias in the data obtained.

It is, therefore, critical to establish a feedback loop to the external data providers to help assure and improve the quality of the data supply.

Example: Airline reservation systems (Sabre, Galileo etc.) provide participating carriers a consolidated data set that is a true record of every single ticket sold through the reservation system. However, this data does not include tickets sold directly through an airlines web site. This could result in under-estimating total market volumes depending on what fraction of total sales happen online. With increasing adoption of online booking, the "missed" portion of the data assumes significant proportions. Additionally, not all carriers have similar Internet booking penetration. Budget and Low Cost airlines choose to sell more tickets on their websites as part of their strategy. This results in a bias of the data that may prove to be insurmountable depending on the intended use.

Survey Tools

In those cases where surveying is conducted in-house, BI tools provide data from a variety of survey questionnaires, the most common being Customer Satisfaction (CSAT) Surveys, Employee Feedback Surveys etc. Survey data is often perceived to be "one-off" and is usually not provisioned for in a BI environment. However, in cases like CSAT, Employee Feedback etc. that are gathered on a regular basis, it is quite useful to understand changing patterns over time and hence necessary to include them in a BI environment.

Other types of Survey data include more generic surveys like Salary Surveys, Lifestyle Surveys etc. that are generally used at aggregated levels to establish broad patterns.

The biggest challenge in including Survey data into a data warehouse is the inability to attach them to the common hierarchies. In specific cases (CSAT, Employees, etc.), such a linkage will exist and is easily used. In the generic case, where responder identities are obfuscated or detail is not captured, such a linkage will have to be created artificially and provisioned for at the time of initiating the survey. For instance: make sure that geographical regions are called out and in line with internal geographical regions at the time of commissioning a lifestyle survey.

Analytical Output

A source of data not generally thought of as a "source" per se, is the output and results of analytics models. Every analytical model generates output—forecasts, predicted probabilities, allocations, etc. that share similar characteristics as the data that was used as input to the model. Yes, indeed model output is often used as input to other models. For instance, output of a forecasting model is used as input to another model that identifies optimal order sizes, which in turn could serve as an input to a third model that identifies optimal freight assignment and so on.

To monitor and control decisions taken with analytical model output, it is critical to test model-predicted values to actual observed values. To enable this comparison, model output should be generated and structured along the same lines and dimensions as source data and fed into the same data storage system. This closed loop enables "monitor and control" that forms a critical component of the decision execution loop and is one of the most critical components that allows for a successful implementation of the analytical framework beyond the traditional BI framework.

Data Loading

Data loading from internal and external databases is used to bring data from multiple disparate repositories into a location that can be shared by many analysts.

Most key business processes in the organization are supported by a tool that has a data repository. Enterprise applications leverage a shared repository that is available to all users, while smaller applications use self-contained repositories (Excel, MS Project etc.). This data has to be captured into a centralized repository or a data warehouse and made available for consumption by Business and analytics. This data is then presented to business users (Presentation) in the form of spreadsheets, reports, dashboards, database views, etc.

In many cases, IT teams work to bring these sets of data into a centralized "data warehouse" that embeds an IT-supported business model to structure the data. This is achieved through two sets of data manipulations:

1. Extract-Transform-Load[4] (ETL) processes that extract data from the source systems, then transform and load them into the data warehouse.

---

[4] Kimball R , Caserta J (2004) The data warehouse ETL toolkit. Wiley, Indianapolis.

2. Database designs[5] in the forms of tables, views, triggers and stored proce-
    dures. The database can be called a data warehouse or a data mart depending
    on its scope and the ambition of its builders.

As a purely IT-managed activity, the quality of the data being loaded cannot be
validated and the best that can be done is to ensure that it tallies with the source
system data. Therefore, the data remains exposed to the vagaries of the various
source systems and the users of these systems. That being said, data gathered
through such IT systems remains the source of highest data fidelity available to the
Analytics Domain.

Solve Data Quality IT Issues

This activity is needed to solve IT-related data problems on an ongoing basis. In
many cases, the IT contact person for this has to figure out if the problem is really
with IT, and if so to route it to the correct IT team and get it addressed. Given
the complexity of the IT infrastructure and organizational structures in most large
companies, this is a formidable task: to work across different IT teams and systems to analyze the root cause (or causes) for a data issue, determine how to solve
it (this is a design or re-design activity), prioritize for development, develop, test,
and deploy the solution.

Problems are minimized in the case where the organization is in stage three of
their BI evolution, where there is no data manipulation in the data arrival stage or
on the way to it. Irreducible concerns continue to stem from the source databases
and their evolution—data quality concerns in the sources stem from and can be
solved by a variety of means, and in this case the BI team needs to collaborate
with the source data system's IT team to work on the solution.

In many cases, this IT complexity leads to the selection of quick-fixes as
opposed to design changes. This further complicates the systems and increases the
costs and cycle time for solving data quality concerns. The BI team gets tempted to
mask the upstream issues by data manipulations in the ETL or BI database design.
This must not be done—if this is done, it generates an implicit model that bypasses
the model management done by the Decision Modeling team and creates the potential for confusion when some unsuspecting analyst trips over this "hidden" model.

Analytical Datasets and BI Assets

A critical component of a BI framework is a data repository that drives all processes and tools that make up the framework. The data repository represents the
single biggest asset of the BI framework and is usually seen as the primary driver

---

[5] http://en.wikipedia.org/wiki/Database_design

behind the BI framework. The data repository comes in several flavors that are often (incorrectly) used interchangeably.

Operational Data Store

An Operational Data Store (ODS) integrates data from disparate sources (through Data Loading). The data is cleaned and rationalized through Data Stewardship to ensure integrity and consistency. An operational data store may be designed to store only a limited history of data with older data flushed periodically into a Data Warehouse. Such operational data stores are sometimes referred to as Staging Databases, since they hold data temporarily before committing it to the Warehouse. Data Store structures are optimized for simple queries with the emphasis on speedy retrieval of limited information.

Data Warehouse

A Data warehouse collects data from operational data stores and stores them for longer term use. A key aspect of a data warehouse is that data is *never* deleted from a warehouse, and once committed to the warehouse, the data becomes a permanent record. Data warehouses are structured to handle complex queries with larger data sets, where speed and responsiveness are often not the driving factor.

A data warehouse is not an essential ingredient for a BI framework, and depending on the volume and usage of the data, a Data Store can effectively serve as a data warehouse for all intents and purposes. In fact a Data Warehouse is so structured that it proves to be a very expensive way to provide BI infrastructure. This is because it creates multiple locations where models must be managed by different specialists: ETL specialists embed data transformations into data flows, Data Warehouse designers put in complex database designs as implicit models, and Business analytics modelers create their own models on top of these and react to business needs by creating overlaps.

Data Mart

A Data Mart is a specialized cut from the data warehouse extracted for very specific business needs. Ownership of these data marts is typically vested with the business units. The business units can use these marts to create ad-hoc dimensions for specific analysis etc. without upsetting the structure of the warehoused data.

Data Marts are also not essential ingredients for BI infrastructure, but get recommended as a "best practice" in most BI implementations as they distribute the management of the Business Analytics Databases. Since it remains the responsibility of decision modeling and decision making functions to take a holistic approach to analytics, the proliferation of data marts simply means that there are more places where models are stored, so more places to manage. To reduce the management overhead, care should be exercised to avoid "Mart Proliferation" which is a result of indiscriminate creation of new data marts for every new business need. Where possible, existing marts should be used or enhanced. A pragmatic approach is to create a single mart for each business unit.

Data Structuring and Transformation

One key process in a BI framework is the transformation and structuring of data into a convenient structure. The choice of structure can be

- Hierarchical Dimensions and Facts—a Star Schema.[6]
- A Normalized Structure—also called a Third Normal Form.[7]

Regardless of the structure chosen, it can either be enforced in the creation of the Operational Data Store and passed on to the Data Warehouse (where appropriate) or enforced in the Data Warehouse with the Operational Data Store remaining unstructured.

It is the recommendation of the authors that the preferred approach will be to enforce structures only in data marts. It is also recommended that the data marts are structured along the Fact-Dimension model (Star Schema) since that is significantly easier for end users to query and use.[8]

Business Analytics Input Databases

The Business Analytics Input Database is an Operational Data Store into which data from various sources flows. The data delivered to this stage must be a faithful representation of data in the source systems. No additional checks are put in place to validate the data available at this stage. The design of this database needs to address how the data is synchronized with its source, and to tune the delay (or cycle time) and data integrity.

It is also possible, sometimes, to look up data as needed from the source systems. This happens when the data source owners allow the BI team to run queries on their "live" data, as opposed to the usual restriction for BI teams to run background low-priority jobs so that the first call on the data is the application that it supports. In this case, it becomes a lot easier to run the data loading (it can be

---

[6] Kimball R (1996) The data warehouse toolkit. Wiley, New York.

[7] Inmon B (1992) Building the data warehouse. Wiley, New York.

[8] A more detailed comparison of the data warehouse structures and the trade-offs can be obtained from Robert Hilliard in his book: Hillard R (2010) Information-driven business. Wiley, New York.

done as needed), but we still need to store the input data in the Input Database. This is required to assure data integrity and data traceability for analytics.

To periodically scrub for data usage and find unused data, it is useful to set up the input database to generate logs and then to mine the log-files to gain insight on data usage.

Business Analytics Ready Databases

A Business Analytics Ready Database is simply a specialized Data Mart upon which analytics models are built. That is because it contains data that has been scrubbed and massaged to meet the analytics needs, and also has access to information about data problems that can be used to forestall incorrect execution of analytics. Examples of such databases include the ubiquitous OLAP[9] cube that is very prevalent in providing reporting and visualization analysis.

The database is primarily created by the outputs from Data Stewardship and Decision Models acting on input data and storing the results in Analytics Ready database.

Here, too, it is useful to set up the database to generate logs and then to mine the log-files to gain insight on how the data is put in and how it is used. This information is useful for both data stewardship and model management.

Analytics Tools

Part of a complete BI framework is a set of analytical tools that are deployed for the analysts to use. There is no shortage of tools available in the market serving various needs and functions supported by a BI framework. Here, we try to call out some key capabilities expected in the toolsets deployed on a BI environment that can assist the reader in making an informed choice of BI tools.

Reporting

BI tools should have the capability for creation of formatted and interactive reports with extensive distribution capabilities. This use of BI tools remains the "Bread and Butter" of BI solutions and careful attention should be paid to the ease of creating and deploying new reports. The ideal tool should also be able to support a wide variety of reporting formats and structures (Graphical, Tabular, Financial, Operational, etc.) and provide the ability to distribute these reports effectively through the web (Intranet) and mobile devices.

---

[9] Online Analytical Processing (OLAP) cube is an array of data that is arranged by multiple dimensions. These are very commonly used in Business Intelligence systems for fast retrieval of organized data grouped and categorized along any on the cubes dimensions.

Dashboards

This is effectively a subset of the Reporting requirement above, but its widespread use merits calling it out separately. The requirements for Dashboards are similar to Reporting, with the emphasis being more on the distribution and visual display of a Dashboard that presents a set of selected metrics in a graphically compelling and usable format. Dashboards are typically consumed by senior management and should be able to communicate critical information effectively and accurately. Edward Tufte has some wonderful insights on the design of dashboards and the ideal tool should be able to implement and adhere to some basic design principles.

Data Visualization

If a picture is worth a thousand words, we can only imagine what effective visualization capabilities are worth ☺ Visualization tools go beyond pretty charts and allow the user to visualize analytical output and what-if scenario evaluation. An effective visualization tool is probably the most powerful weapon in the arsenal of the analyst, since it can communicate advanced concepts and complex interactions very effectively, in a fashion that makes it easy for the non-technical business user to understand the analytical output. In fact, lack of effective visualization capabilities remains one of the reasons for lack of "buy-in" into analytics. An effective visualization removes the dependence on the individual analyst to communicate the power of analytical models.

Modeling Capabilities

Another essential arrow in the BI quiver is the ability to build analytical models quickly and effectively. The ability to build statistical and optimization models quickly enables the analyst to explore and leverage a larger scope of the analytical knowledge base, and choose the modeling approach or technique best suited for the problem at hand. Slow and cumbersome modeling exercises result in suboptimal model selection and loss of "trust" in the analytical output.

Spreadsheets and Microsoft Office Integration

After all that is said and done, Microsoft Excel remains the single most popular and common tool for quick and basic analysis. It goes without saying that for a BI platform to gain acceptance it should cater to the needs of the single most popular consumption medium.

Data Stewardship and Meta Data Management

This BI function has been gaining importance and focus of late. As databases grow in size and complexity, it is critical to have effective data management practices in place to allow the users to effectively search for and find the exact data they are looking for. One could get away without this function in the past, but as more and more data is handled in the BI framework, the importance of this capability can only increase.

Collaboration

This feature allows users of the BI platform to share and discuss information, analysis, model results, manage hierarchies via discussion threads, embedded annotations, comments and recommendations. The tool should enable this capability through multiple channels including chat, social software, screen sharing etc. This is another feature that is gaining importance rapidly especially considering the geographically distributed teams that are very common today.

Inline Analytics Tools Deployment

All the analytical tools described in the previous section are, by their very nature, geared for an Offline mode of operation. Offline refers to the fact that the model output is not consumed in real time, but rather to aid in human decision making. Depending on the source of data used for these models (Operational Data Source, Data Mart, Data Warehouse, Source System data), the data used by the model could be in real time, or stale by the frequency of the ETL process that feeds the source BI asset. While such offline use of analytical models is sufficient in most cases, there do arise specific business needs where Analytical model output needs to be consumed in real-time.

Credit Card fraud detection process is an example of such real time analytical output need. As credit card transaction requests are registered, analytical models are used to identify potentially fraudulent transactions.

The nature of analytical models, however, is that performance of model evaluation generally cannot be *guaranteed* to be within the necessary thresholds to support real time decision making. Furthermore, since the transactional systems that consume these results in real time are independent of the BI framework, it is not possible for them to know about the nature of the model that will be used to evaluate transactions. An acceptable compromise has been to encapsulate the decision model output into "rules" that can be followed effectively and quickly by the transaction evaluation system in real-time. These rules are recalibrated and reset periodically using offline analytical tools. The frequency of refresh of these rules is driven by the business need. These rules are pushed into a Data Mart for exclusive use by the transaction processing system

Historical credit card transactions are analyzed to identify patterns on known fraudulent transactions. For instance, transactions above $500 on jewelry purchases in a particular region could be identified as "High Risk" on possible fraud. This would then be loaded as a rule into the OLTP, and when such a transaction is encountered, the OLTP would alert an agent to seek additional confirmation (Call the card user for instance) before approving the transaction. This reduces the occurrence of fraud on these types of transactions. The analysis is repeated periodically to identify other such rules and the rules Data Mart is updates regularly. This allows the OLTP to consume the result of analytical modeling "Inline" or in "real time". While a true "Real Time" system would actually run a scoring algorithm to evaluate the probability of fraud, the scoring algorithm is currently too expensive (time consumption) to be deployed inline. Such a "true" real time analytical model consumption would most certainly be superior to the rule based approach used today, but would need significant changes in the OLTP system to be able to use a scoring algorithm (that can change dynamically) as well is improvements in technology to enable scoring algorithms to evaluate thousands and millions of transactions in a time frame that is acceptable to be deployed in real-time.

Chapter 8
Data Stewardship: Can We Use the Data?

Before you consume data for analyses, first assess it. Data sets may contain problems that can make the analysis incorrect and the recommendations misleading. This generally happens the first time the data is used for analysis, and also periodically and randomly disrupts ongoing analyses on pre-established data flows when something changes upstream or in the analytics infrastructure. The price of good data is eternal vigilance ☺.

Data stewardship is a set of activities that convert input (raw) data into data that is usable for analytics (Fig. 8.1).

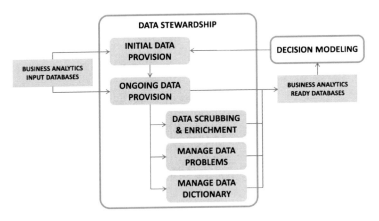

Fig. 8.1 Data stewardship

Initial Data Provision

This starts with a new data request needed to make a Decision Model. This can be a new data-set or related to a different use-case for existing data. For instance, you may already be providing project data to track margin, but have not used the data

R. Saxena and A. Srinivasan, *Business Analytics*, International Series in Operations
Research & Management Science 186, DOI: 10.1007/978-1-4614-6080-0_8,
© Springer Science+Business Media New York 2013

to check project delays, which requires accuracy in date-fields that were earlier not used for analysis. In general, whenever you look at a dataset for the first time you find it filled with garbage because unless data is used its integrity is not regarded highly by anybody who does data entry or IT jobs.

The Analytics Data Steward needs to figure out how to satisfy the need. As the data request is new, the Steward has to work with the Modeling analyst to understand the data needs, think of likely data sources, and may try to think of alternate data sets. You need to get a data set, and review it to assess if it fits the analytics need.

First-Cut Review of the Data

Since the data set is often the result of a query or a set of queries, and sometimes later processing in a spreadsheet, the first order of business is to test for querying and spreadsheet errors.

1. Count the records. Do you see round numbers of rows like 2000, 5000, 2400? Often round numbers result from the IT analyst trying to limit the data-set size to a "representative sample". Is that what you needed?
2. Add up columns to see if the data looks complete. For example you can add up the project time consumed column and check it against the timecards filed in the timecard data to ensure that all the project data has flowed into your data set. This cross-checking step also checks for data completeness.
3. Look for mistakes in lookups and joins, or cut/paste artifacts. This can be done by following a row through all its columns, or look for nulls and try to see if they make sense.
4. In the columns that behave like a list of values, look at the values to see if the values correspond to your expectations. For example, a Project ID column should contain entries that conform to your company's format, or columns that should contain dates should have date entries, etc. Look out for fake numbers, like all the same digit (99999 or 111-11-1111)—people put in such data when the system forces them to enter data and they don't want to.
5. Bounce the data against a trusted data-set that has some of the same columns. For example, check your untrusted project data versus your trusted headcount report. Do all the people in the project data belong to the headcount data? Are both datasets consistent in labeling employees and contractors?

Sorts, Scatters and Histograms

1. Look at the top and bottom entries. For example, sort order data by value and look at the names of the customers. Do they make sense?
2. Visualize time-series data. You may have asked for last month's booking data, in which case the time-stamps should run throughout that time period with no

    suspicious gaps. Sort by time-stamps; look at top and bottom entries, as well as spikes (too many bookings in a time-period) and dips (few or no bookings). Do they correspond to your needs and expectations?
3.   Scatter or categorize the data along any two selected columns to see if the data conforms to your expectations. Categorize sales by region to check if there are any missing regions. A scatter for cost-per-hour of a resource versus the days (timeline versus $-cost/hour) should not vary much by time. A scatter of project budgeted cost versus actual cost can be expected to have a pattern in which budgets align to actuals—in this case a lack or pattern will trigger you to look deeper to eliminate data-sourcing artifacts. There should be no customer-billable hours logged against pre-sales projects, and very few non-billable hours on billable (booked) projects. The sales figures for countries are likely to be correlated with the GDP.
4.   Make histograms of key values, like project duration or cost per employee. They generally follow a pattern, such as a Normal or a Poisson distribution. If you do not see the expected distribution, look deeper.

Fitness for Use

The next step is to check for value-add—the data needs to be useful for an analytics model. Are important data elements available as needed? Is the data going to be available in the volume you need for analysis?

    Data stewards also concern themselves about whether the data is true. Credit card transaction data comes from machine-reading of the credit card identifiers and the amounts put in by the seller are verified by the buyer at the point of sale. Weekly timecard data is put in by people who are expected to accurately track and record the actual time they spent at work during the week. Data stewards think about how to design the data collection and data flows so that errors do not creep in. They also need to find errors, track and control them, and help data users understand the data errors and possibly how to compensate for them.

    In many cases, the modeler expects to see data conform to standard distributions. The arrival rates of calls into a call center are expected to be a Poisson distribution, failure rates correspond to the Weibull distribution, and measurement errors look like a Normal distribution. The Data Steward should make histograms of the data and if you do not see the distributions you expect, then first test for and eliminate data errors. In case the deviations (non-standard or multimodal distributions) persist as true reflections of reality, the modelers need to be informed and they are likely to improve their model.

    Verify the data against its source, as intermediate systems introduce invisible errors. Check the integrity of data feeds from the source system to assess if you can assure data integrity. If possible, also check for the reputation of the data source—you may find, for instance, that some data sources are known to have unverified or corrupt data.

Check if the data-set can be provided or accessed on an ongoing basis. Find out about access rights and data security requirements. Determine how fresh or delayed the data feed will be.

Privacy and Surveillance

It is now possible to observe, record, and collate data that can threaten your privacy and serve as the foundation for a surveillance society. The Data Steward can ensure that the data available for use in analytics is fit for use in business analytical models, and not indiscriminately available to analysts for purposes that could breach privacy.

In one sense, this is an easy requirement to add—it's already hard enough to satisfy the data needs for analytical models, and all we ask is to limit the data to those needs. The tricky part is that the Data Stewards need to understand if a model breaches privacy, and also whether different models can be combined to collate a model that can breach privacy. While safeguarding privacy is a wider responsibility, data availability is the hinge point for attackers and lawsuits.

Ongoing Data Provision

After an analytics model has proved to be useful and required on an ongoing basis, it generally needs access to refreshed data. To ensure that the data remains of sufficient quality in the data used for analyses, we need to set up ongoing provision of data.

Ongoing Data Sourcing

To set up, maintain, and shut down data feeds into the Data Arrival Stage, we use the Ongoing Data Sourcing function to manage data flows. In this work you become familiar with the complexities of Extract, Transform, and Loading (ETL) tools and the various issues that make so-called automated data flows into fragile human-supported procedures. Where there is an effect on the accuracy and timeliness of the data, this learning should be transferred to the Ongoing Data Assessment function.

You are also subjected to the effects of system design changes in source systems on the data flowing to you. To insulate yourself from such changes you may be tempted to insert code (transformations) into the data flow into the Data Arrival Stage. Resist this temptation. Ensure that all data transformations are conducted in one place, by a Data Scrubbing & Data Enrichment function. This makes all data issues visible and manageable by one function. We have often found Data

Stewards working hard to figure out the data transformations encoded by an ETL implementation team that lead to unexpected data issues—entirely avoidable if you never put transforms inside the data sourcing data flows.

Ongoing Data Assessment

This function checks incoming data against the existing data, and monitors for variances such as:

- Data loss: we may expect that in general everyone files timecards every week, and see a mean and standard deviation for the number of timecards filed. In case the incoming data exceeds the upper or lower control limits on that data, you can trigger an alert. This alerting can be in conjunction with or independent of whether a control chart[1] is actually set up for the data quality monitoring.
- We expect certain data values to be in certain formats. We can run queries to assure that, or trigger alerts.
- We expect lists of values and hierarchies to be maintained in a consistent manner between the analytics and data-source systems. This can be tested by comparing the new data feed to existing master data, and to flag unexpected changes. For example an upstream system may have created a new department that may not exist in the analytics system, and as a result the analytics for the new department may not get created (or reflect incorrectly).
- Data may be expected to show up every night. In case the schedule is missed, we could run a piece of code to alert us of this and enable corrective action to be taken.

Ongoing data stewardship practices are needed as foundational in case the organization demands service level agreements (SLA) from the analytics team. Analytics SLA depend on IT to supply data on an SLA, and ongoing checking assures the quality and timeliness of the data supply.

With increasingly large volumes of data becoming available, we also need to watch out for the point at which it becomes unavoidable to use greater automation for this function or risk it getting swept away in a flood of unreliable data that the function is unable to process fast enough.

Data Scrubbing and Enrichment

This function changes the data to make it better suited for analytics. To maintain traceability it is best to append the changed data as opposed to overwriting the original data. The new data created by Data Stewards can be called "scrubbed"

---

[1] http://en.wikipedia.org/wiki/Control_chart

or "enriched". Data scrubbing and enrichment incorporates analysts' opinions into the data for use in the analyses.

Data Scrubbing

Data scrubbing makes facts clearer: incoming data generally needs to be scrubbed to make it ready for use in analyses. Some columns may need to be dropped, as being misleading or containing garbage. Other columns may contain cryptic codes that we replace with understandable data that maintains the same or similar meaning. We may delete rows of data as being meaningless noise, and other rows as being outliers. The trick with data scrubbing is to have as little scrubbing as possible. We should make a "high fidelity" dataset and let the analysts who make Decision Models use the full dataset and make decisions on what to include or exclude (as noise or outliers) depending on the needs of the model.

A widespread problem addressed in data scrubbing is to clean up data entry errors in fields such as those used for names, addresses, and phone numbers. This is used to correct the data (name, address, etc.) for the customer, supplier, employee, etc. Sometimes the correction may not be as trivial as correcting a typo—it can require us to distinguish between similar names and typos, translations of local languages and native scripts, etc. Correcting names can lead to de-duplication of records, when we find one correct name can stand-in for multiple related instances, and this scrubbing process is sometimes called de-duping or matching. Re-formatting the data to follow a convention, as for telephone numbers in the USA, is called "parsing and standardization". The dataset that results from matching, parsing, and standardization is often called a "master" (like a Customer Master, Supplier Master, etc.) and the management of these "master" datasets has its very own acronym: Master Data Management (MDM).[2] MDM systems are used to connect data from different systems to provide "enterprise wide" views. The errors and judgment calls built-into these views are outweighed by the larger benefits from correctly matching most of the records. These benefits are sustained and amplified by integrating MDM into processes that enable or dictate the maximum reuse of the master data, and govern its quality.

Data Enrichment

Data enrichment is included as a Data Stewardship function to enable sharing of analyst-generated data. In the world of business analytics, the analysts create models and uses for data and generate useful results in their models. These results can

---

[2] http://en.wikipedia.org/wiki/Master_data_management

be written back into the analytics database for use by other analysts, and they are called data enrichments—they are really "opinions" created by the analysts.

Some of these enrichments can be created by hand, such as manually tagging bookings as being related to a particular technology solution based on the analyst collecting the opinions of the relevant sales teams.

In many cases, the enrichment is generated by an algorithm. These algorithms run in the database and record the results into an enrichment column or table. The algorithm that generates the results can be simple or complex, access data from other datasets, incorporate deep expertise, and have built-in learning. An example of an opinion is the likelihood of an opportunity to get closed, the likelihood of fraud in a sale, or the chances that a loan will go bad.

We can also enrich the data by connecting it to other related datasets that combine to provide more information. A business customer record can be matched to a node in a customer master hierarchy purchased from a third party provider such as Dun & Bradstreet or Experian to provide creditworthiness information, or a person's name can be matched to the records in databases from providers such as Acxiom, TransUnion or Equifax to get the person's credit score and credit history.

In some cases we summarize data, in others we may end up exploding it into more detail and enriching it with information from another dataset. When data is exploded (e.g., when we mix summary and detail data to generate a more meaningful detail data-set) we often find data that exists at the summary level is not there at the detail we have created as it may be missing in related detail datasets. In these cases we may choose to "stuff" data by copying it down from the summary layer or applying rules such as interpolation or weighted allocation.

Sometimes we find that some data is missing, either randomly or systematically. A set of countries may have different periodicities in collecting data such as for education or diseases, so the dataset across countries and years will have missing values. Survey-takes may not fill in responses to some questions, or surveys may systematically be designed to ask a different set of 20 questions from a bank of 40 questions. Missing data is a common problem and people use various methods to deal with it.[3] There are statistical techniques that generate values for missing data.[4]

It is not necessary to tightly control the number of data enrichments. It is useful for the Data Stewards to review enrichments and to foster the reuse of existing enrichments. In many cases we find analysts engaged in enriching the data in similar ways, and we get a huge improvement in consistency and productivity when the Data Stewards get them to agree to use the same enrichment. This endeavor is supported by the creation and maintenance of a Data Dictionary that contains all the enrichments supported by the Data Stewards.

In all cases, any dataset constitutes a composite opinion made up of the source data and the enrichments. Its governance by Data Stewards needs to include

---

[3] http://en.wikipedia.org/wiki/Missing_data

[4] Enders CK (2010) Applied missing data analysis. Guildford Press, New York.

methods for error correction. Check your own credit history that credit reporting companies maintain—you may find a personal need for data-error correction
processes.

On Hierarchies, Tagging, and Categorizations

Business Analysts love using hierarchies to organize data. They do this to mimic
the hierarchical structure of most organizations, and then add more hierarchies
to categorize and subdivide data. Learning to use the analytics database often
involves using the hierarchy cheat-sheet, to help you navigate the multidimen-
sional data-space created by your fellow analysts. We also put tags and categories onto data, and these can be considered to be hierarchies with just one level.
Adding hierarchy and category data is the most common form of data enrichment.
   It is common to encounter these hierarchies:

- Time Period: starts from the time-stamp on the record to build a hierarchy of
  periods—Day, Week, Month, Quarter, and Year (Calendar year or Fiscal year).
- Customer's Geographic Location: this starts from address data such as zip code,
  city, or country and generally uses company-specific territory hierarchies such
  as North America, Latin America, EMEA (that bundles Europe, Africa, the
  Middle East, and sometimes Russia and the CIS countries), APAC (that often
  includes Australia, China, South Asia, etc.). In some cases the customer name or
  salesperson name may be used to determine the customer geographic location.
- Line of Business: starts from the particular product, service, or solution and
  builds up into the major lines-of-business such as Hardware, Software, Services,
  and Finance.
- Customer Industry: such as Automotive, Retail, Municipal, Banking, etc.

   Think of services delivery data—it can have additional hierarchies such as:

- The Financial Owner for the service: starts from the name of the delivery owner's department and climbs up the chain of departments.
- Skills required for the service: starts from the skills called out for each task to
  connect to a hierarchy of skills.

   We also "tag" services with labels to depict dimensions such as

- Service Type: Advice, Implementation, Operation, Break/Fix, Critical Situation,
  etc.
- Customer Account Coverage Model: Large Account (has a Sales Team),
  Assigned Account (has an assigned salesperson), other (no assigned salesperson), etc.

   Tags and hierarchies are opinions about categorizations that can carry huge
business significance: my sales quota achievement is measured by the sales transactions tagged to my node in the hierarchy, or my sales contracts must be entered

into the system before midnight to count as having occurred in this quarter. As with any categorization scheme, they also suffer from being:

- **Arbitrary**: it is rare to find unambiguous dividing lines between categories except for physical dimensions such as time. Other dimensions are set with some measure of arbitrariness—e.g., a customer can be tagged to an industry based on a sales team's opinion, or by considering the preponderance of their revenues. Say a multinational company headquartered in India directs its subsidiary in Ethiopia to buy a tractor from Caterpillar—the Caterpillar analyst could assign the sale to its India sales territory because they were responsible for the sale or to its Ethiopian territory to record where its tractor went and the customer entity that paid for it.
- **Changeable**: hierarchies and tags periodically change, for instance a sales territory hierarchy can be revised by organizational changes in the sales teams, we can change the Coverage Model for an account, etc.
- **Confusing**: hierarchies can look similar but mean different things. Consulting and Sales teams may be organized using different hierarchies (it is rare to find two organizations with a one-to-one correspondence in their hierarchy) and so they will each separately tag the same order into their own hierarchy, and so we'll find two hierarchies that look similar but carry different business meanings.
- **Intertwined**: different data-points are used to set membership in different hierarchies, and so a sales order with three line-items can be tagged at the order-level to a sales hierarchy but at the line-item level to lines of business. Committed ship dates may be different for each line-item (same day, after a week, etc.) which can put the revenue forecasts for the same order into different time-buckets.

Arbitrary, changeable, confusing, intertwined … and it gets more complex when you move upstream or downstream in the business process and encounter *interconnected* analytics requirements that demand different categorizations. The Sales-oriented hierarchy for customer industry can be different from customer categorizations used for marketing analysis by our Marketing department, which may differ from research conducted by an external marketing analyst, but we can benefit from combining the marketing and sales data to drive sales territory design. When we need to bridge from one hierarchy to another, the Quality Function Deployment (QFD) method[5] from the realm of Quality Management provides an example of how to build such bridges. QFD is widely used in product development analyses, e.g., to relate customer needs to product features.

Inconsistency gets flagged when different analysts use confusingly similar hierarchies or categories to mean different things. Meetings get derailed when people are unable to decide which data to believe. To avoid such confusion and possible obfuscation, it is best to nominate the "official" hierarchies and tags that are to be

---

[5] http://en.wikipedia.org/wiki/Quality_function_deployment

used. The responsibility for keeping the hierarchies current can be pinned on specific owners who set up the governance processes needed to keep the hierarchies accurate. Stewardship of hierarchies or categories makes for consistent analytics—but people should not confuse consistency with truth.

The stewardship process needs to maintain hierarchies and categories so that they do reflect the truth as closely as possible. Hierarchies and category data must not be allowed age into obsolescence. In addition to keeping up with business changes as organizations evolve (e.g., change their sales organization, add a product, etc.), the analyst should enable proactive changes. An analyst with an idea should be able to make a data "enrichment" with a new hierarchy or category, and as with any experiment we can learn from its benefits as well as from its deficiencies. Benefits can be moved into the "official" hierarchies as part of the data stewardship. In this way we provide consistency in analytics and also foster evolution.

Manage Data Problems

In the Initial Data Assessment, we often find critical problems that can impair the analyticsor represent opportunities for improvement. It is the Data Stewards' responsibility to solve the data problems.

For each data problem, we size its effect (this information is used to prioritize its solution), assess the root cause, drive corrective action, and then set up preventive measures. Finally, after the corrective and preventive steps, we continue to monitor the problem.

During their lifecycle, the data problems are placed in different buckets for different groups to address, e.g., users of a certain application, the IT team that does data loads, an IT team that creates interfaces or another that maintains a source application, an outsourced sales operations team, the business policies team, etc. We need to manage the data problems so as to keep track of the problems, prioritize and drive corrective actions by disparate teams, and to communicate progress so that solved problems result in more impactful analytics.

It is useful to put up charts and dashboards to track and communicate the status of data problems. We can draw an analogy with the "bugs and maintenance" management work required for any business application of IT, except that in this case the scope includes IT and business issues.

Work with IT to Solve IT Issues

For IT, handling a data problem has to be addressed as part of the IT support processes. These processes are often cost constrained, and often outsourced. Case trackers are used for this purpose, and analysts learn to doggedly pursue their cases in the face of multi-tiered support processes.

A "best practice" for IT is to assign dedicated data stewards to work with their counterparts in the analytics team. This partnership proves very useful both to solve some "low hanging fruit" data problems quickly and effectively, and also to help other IT teams to get engaged.

Work with Business to Solve Business Issues

Business people are not used to having analysts come back and tell them about how they need to change their ways to help the organization to use analytics better … but this is required. Data Stewards need to work with their business counterparts to solve business issues that impair the analytics, such as policies, training, user errors, etc.

User Errors: Many data problems are caused by user error that results in bad data input. We have seen cases where the solution to bad data entry upstream is to have another set of people work on cleaning up the bad data downstream. This is unproductive, we prefer to improve the initial data quality… and initial data quality never improves unless you tell people about their data input mistakes and teach them how (and why) to fix them.

We can set up an automated feedback loop to send alerts about data-input problems back to the people who put the bad data in. This loop has proven to be a "best practice" that eliminates rework downstream and also inculcates greater concern and awareness for data quality in the organization.

Training: Business people need training to learn about the value of clean data and to help them think about how to create and use the data assets in their organization. It is not clear to many people that data assets are valuable, and how they are used in business.

Business Policies: People who set business policies may have little understanding of how they interlock with other policies. Analytics often reveals the issues as analysts try to weave a broader picture, and then it becomes the Data Stewards' problem to solve the policy-related issues. In one case we found a policy that expenses could not be tagged to a project after the project was closed out, and this policy was at odds with the employee expense policy and the vendor billing policy that allowed expenses to be claimed or procured services to be billed months after they were incurred. So project-related expenses logged after the project was closed out could not be "officially" tagged to the project, leaving a substantial amount of cost as invisible. This missing cost was located after we started to tag all expenses to projects.

Manage Data Dictionary

A data dictionary is used to describe what data is available, how it is structured, where it came from (trace to sources, record transformations, scrubs, and enrichments), and provides guidance on how it can be used. It includes the knowledge of data problems—the current state and the track record of fixes. It is best to use the dictionary both as a snapshot of the current situation and as a history of how the system evolved.

Analysts use the data dictionary to find and use data for their models, and to determine if data that they need is actually missing or too "dirty" to use (in the sense of containing data errors). In the data dictionary they should find:

- Clear and unambiguous data element definition, including what it means, format, and size
- Guidance on how it can be used, where or how it is currently used, or if it has fallen to disuse (superseded by another data element). In secured-access databases, we can mine the data access logs to describe and track usage of data.
- Trace to sources or origins
- Record of transformations, scrubs, and enrichments
- Knowledge of data problems—data quality issues (open or closed), the track record of fixes, and links to see the current state of data quality
- Last update date of the data, the data-dictionary entry, and last-verified date, to help the analyst understand if the data and its dictionary entry might be stale.

While making and maintaining the data dictionary, we find data issues to resolve:

- Locate, flag, and eliminate duplicate or overlapping elements and drive consistent usage
- Show which source systems provide data traceability, measure data quality by source, etc.—this visibility helps the source system owners to solve the highlighted issues
- Locate old data and old data-dictionary entries that can be in need of verification, provide a last-verified date and signature to certify validity.

Chapter 9
Making Organizations Smarter

This chapter deals with how to propagate an "analytics culture" in the organization. Such a culture is required to enable the successful use of analytics, and its absence retards or stalls the use of analytics. You may think that companies would naturally embed analytics into their work culture, but think about it—analytics people come from a mathematics and quantitative background but everyone does not, and many of those with a quantitative backgrounds let those skills and approaches fall into disuse as their day-to-day work teaches them to get by without.

The idea is to help you collaborate with your business counterparts to get their alignment use analytics in the decision cycle—to use it, use it repeatedly, and to make it a habit and culture.

Why Bother with Analytics?

If the idea is to help the organization behave smarter, do we need "Business Analytics" for it?

The us of business analytics provides the attractive prospect of being able to become more successful in business. It can help improve results by scientifically deploying the resources, or to get to the same goals with fewer resources. It holds out the prospect of tightly aligning strategy with execution, and of making organizations survive longer because they adapt faster to the changing business ecosystem.

There are recent publications that correlate business performance with the use of analytics[1] and there is widespread belief that analytics should help improve performance. This belief takes support from the tradition of quantitative approaches to management that are taught in business schools and widely used in practice.

---

[1] MIT Sloan Management Review and the IBM Institute for Business Value (2010) Analytics: The new path to value, MIT Sloan Management Review Research Report Fall 2010.

R. Saxena and A. Srinivasan, *Business Analytics*, International Series in Operations Research & Management Science 186, DOI: 10.1007/978-1-4614-6080-0_9, © Springer Science+Business Media New York 2013

Quantitative branches of management have a huge knowledge-base of analytics techniques and examples where value was derived from their use. Professional societies and businesses draw from and add to this knowledgebase on an ongoing basis. This data shows how the application of analytics has led to benefits, and leads us to think that the ongoing use of analytics is beneficial, so our rational response is to proceed on this hypothesis as being well-supported and the best guide to action that we have.

Repeated and propagated analytics behaviors can get built into a culture that naturally uses analytics. Such a culture will foster curiosity, teach exploration, and reward both innovation and the teamwork that moves the organization towards its goals. It will also be creative, objective and inclusive. These are good attributes to have in a workgroup.

The knowledgebase for analytics is vast, there are lots of analytics tools, thousands of experts, and ever-present salesmen—so you should always be able to get ideas on how to use analytics in your specific case. Analytics not only generates more money (may be too dry), but its use provides access to lots of cool technologies, pretty charts, and (of late) much good press. You can get rich, famous, and look good as you play with analytics—put a chicken in every pot and a dashboard with blinking lights on every screen ☺

Analytics Culture Maturity

It is seldom the case that analytics is never used in the organization—decisions are made on a day to day basis and these decisions are based in some rational decision making model using various tangible and in-tangible inputs. What we are looking for is an end state where every decision is driven through the rigor of an analytical framework and the decisions are repeatable, scalable, rational, and data driven.

To drive an organization towards Analytics Culture Maturity, we start by identifying where the organization stands today. Think about how readily your business colleagues use analytics. Rate each of them on a five-point scale:

1. Unaware of how analytics can be used
2. Aware of analytics but do not use it for various reasons (not available, poor quality, cannot trust or understand the analytics, etc.)
3. Use analytics when it is available
4. Support the creation and usage of analytics
5. Leader in using analytics, recognize applicability, and demand the best analytics.

Aggregate the results. At stage 5 we have an analytics culture, and analytics behaviors are modeled and propagated as a matter of course. In earlier stages the use of analytics is exhibited, maybe even repeated and supported, but not entrenched.

Based on the maturity, analysts can determine how to foster the analytics culture. Assess and communicate its value to the organization. Enable more people to see the value of analytics, use it, and communicate how they used it and benefited.

We often encounter the fake analytics culture—one where people say they use analytics but in reality the analytics are either:

- flawed, such that the analytics cannot support rational decision making, and force people to use non-analytical methods (like guessing, gut feel, or the "sense" of the team, etc.) or
- political, where analytics is used as a veneer for an underlying non-objective method.

In this case the journey becomes much more difficult—if the self-stated maturity is higher than the observed maturity, analysts face greater difficulty in getting people to invest in the quality of analytics that is actually needed. The push-back will be that "we already have it", and there may be people vested into defending why the analytics are "good" or (more insidiously) "good enough".

Depending on the organization's maturity and culture, analysts should propose methods to improve its use of analytics. Several consulting firms position their proprietary pathways to maturity. Some organizations like to proceed in a planned manner, others pilot and scale. Decide whether to lead or follow, build or buy, rent or own. Go enterprise-wide or silo in scope, centralized or distributed in execution, etc.

Paths can themselves be subjected to analytics—to assess the baseline and select the options. Barriers to change in the baseline case are different at different levels:

1. Unaware of how analytics can be used in their team. In this case, there is either:
    a. no awareness—so we need to create awareness of the possibilities from analytics or shock them awake by showing how competition is using analytics to win
    b. no case for change—where we need to show the path to and size the returns on the investment in analytics, and (where possible) show how their peers leverage analytics—often a related department in the same company has started using analytics
    c. cost perception—in cases where people may think that analytics is too costly. This perception is bolstered by press about the need for huge IT investments in data warehouses and expensive analysts. We need to show how analytics comes at many scales, from free (do it yourself to hugely expensive.

2. Aware of analytics but do not use it for various reasons
    a. analytics skills may not be available
    b. data quality could stymie the analysts
    c. the organization does not have data available (data access can be blocked by IT, or managers may not pay for data to be collected)

    d.   people lack the skills to understand and confidence to act on the analytics

    e.   tried and failed (lack of proven value from analytics investments or a history of failure with analytics projects)—in this case the team needs to rework its path and rebuild its confidence in analytics.

3. Use analytics when it is available—where the use of analytics is spotty, we encounter

    a.   data access, data quality, and data governance problems

    b.   lack of management attention due to competing priorities or lack of consistent executive sponsorship

    c.   culture that discourages info sharing

    d.   turf battles over the ownership of data, of the analytics teams, funding, technology, etc.

4. Support the creation and usage of analytics—here the stakes are bigger as analytics grows in size and scope

    a.   battles about ownership and governance (control) of the analytics assets

    b.   periodic inquisitions into the "value of analytics"(often launched by sponsors of competing priorities)

    d.   funding issues

    e.   running out of ideas on what to do next.

5. Leader in using analytics—in this case the march of analytics leadership periodically gets impeded when it encounters a period of chaos that disables the finely tuned analytics. This pushes the organization into a lower state of maturity and requires rebuilding its analytics assets.

Actionable Analytics

Regardless of the path to maturity, the moment of truth for analytics is when its recipient decides to use it … or not. The objective, of course, is for people to use the analytics to make and execute decisions. For this to happen, the analytics must be "actionable":

- Suggest the action to be taken, or rate/rank options (explicitly or implicitly where the paths are clearly understood already)
- Be confident in making the recommendation—for this, the analyst must be able to assess confidence intervals on the findings and recommendations, be sure about the quality of the model, and have a firm grasp of the data quality.

    The requirement for analytics to be actionable must be tested against the reality of whether a particular recommendation (or report) is actually acted upon. Actionable is an opinion. Action taken is fact. Test if your report is read, look for the resulting actions and test for the results. What you find will reveal if the analytics are useful.

What should you do if the analytics are not useful, or not useful enough to justify the cost? You can reduce cost or increase the value. Reducing costs can come from using technologies such as self-service reports or dashboards … technologies you should review anyway. To increase value you can rework the model, work with decision-makers on how to use the model more effectively, or with decision execution to drive results and refine the model.

Measure the Value of Analytics

When you use analytics to understand the need to act, to evaluate courses of action, and to steer towards your goal, you are "driving with the headlights on". This is not a common experience for business persons, who often describe their jobs as struggling with avoidable uncertainties. The experience makes the business person become a supporter of analytics. Even if it seems superfluous, it is still useful to measure the value realized and value leakages, because it:

1. Continuously tests that the model is valuable (that it is actionable, acted upon, and provides results)
2. Illuminates opportunities for ongoing improvement, and the gap between value potential and realization
3. Enables the model to be refined and improved iteratively (provides data to test if the refinements improve or detract)
4. Tracks value realized overall, to buttress the analytics culture.

Value measurements are different for different types of analytics.

- **Offensive Analytics** capture value—say by better targeting of customers to increase market penetration or wallet-share, or by squeezing money out of the supply chain. In these cases you can assess value realized.
- **Defensive Analytics** protect against leakages that occur on the journeys from idea to results or to defend against counterattacks in the time you protect your results against market reactions. In these cases you model stage-wise value:
    - Value potential identified (addressable market), targeted (addressed market), leaked and captured.
    - Value at risk, lost and defended.

- **Ancillary Analytics** such as customer satisfaction or consultant utilization rates are used as input to offensive and defensive models, and do not inherently lead to value. As such they are part of the cost base and we may allocate the cost of these analytics to the value-creating analytics.

The measurement of value from analytics is generally structured as a "natural experiment" model. It is rare to find cases where the use of analytics is structured as a proper scientific experiment with effective randomization and controls.

After you measure value, communicate it so that it continually reinforces the analytics culture—the culture of driving with headlights, of making decisions from data.

Scaling the Decision Culture

As the analytics culture takes root and finds support, we can think about scaling it widely. Ask yourself: how can we help all our people make better decisions?

First, teach people how to use analytics in their work, and to want to do so. A good analogy is with the widespread use of "Quality Circles" in manufacturing industries. To do this, analysts will need to work not just with fellow analysts and senior management but also with a greater number and variety of people. Sometimes these people may be outside the company, such as customers or suppliers who participate in the analytics ecosystem. For example, a large retailer can benefit from teaching all its suppliers about how to integrate with the retailer's sales analytics.

Second, scale intelligence by embedding rules into workflows, as discussed in the workflow layer models. The concern here is that as the organization "learns" it often adds more rules. Over time, obsolete rules become encrustations that are difficult to locate because of their tiny and insidious effects. We already have lots of unwritten and written rules governing our workflows. To this we add analytics rules-bases. With bigger and more complex rules embedded in the rules-bases, it becomes harder to understand the workflow and to evolve it. The only defense against encrustation and ossification (death by creeping rules) is to periodically test the validity of each rule or analytics model.

Lies, Damn Lies and Statistics (or Analytics)

The difficult part comes when you find extraneous factors such as decision biases, deception or irrationality have leached away the value. In many cases models are misused to provide a fig leaf of data to support off-model behavior, and this is a corruption of analytics that poisons the perception of analytics. These misuses must be addressed or the model discontinued and disavowed.

It gets more complex when different analysts address the same concern using different models to arrive at divergent conclusions. Such clashing models are often seen in debates between departments, between experts from different schools of thought, or from politicians of differing ideologies. The different value of alternate approaches may only appear in the long run, and often the criteria and weights also differ. Analysts need to fold these models into their multi-criteria multi-scenario multi-model world … and this shifts the problem into the Decision Making function where it belongs, and where the Advisor must grapple with it.

Value Management: From Assessment to Realization

A constant criticism of analytics is its apparent disconnect from operational realities and lack of measurable and tangible impact of "esoteric" models. This is often cited as an outcome of the analyst not "understanding the business" and building models that are not grounded in reality. The analytics framework established in this book will address those concerns significantly by ensuring that the analysis is well grounded in business and decision needs and the stakeholders are kept engaged to understand what to expect from the analysis.

However, analytics can still fail due to operational considerations in converting the perceived benefits of the decision model into operational reality. While management support to drive data driven decision making is a critical ingredient in making it work, there are steps that can be built into ensure an easy and seamless implementation of analytical decision making.

Make a Plan

Design a "Target State" that has a decision model aligned with the business strategy. Use the model to define critical metrics and balancing metrics to create an interlocking set of metrics. Use the target state definition to provide the frame within which to baseline the current state (a baseline without a target-frame is an open-ended exercise or arbitrary). Such a plan will align the stakeholders on the ultimate benefits without being side-tracked on minor considerations and falling prey to the various irrationality traps identified in the book.

Armed with the target state, define the roadmap of projects to get to the target state. The plan is also exposed to the stakeholders, including the expected time for implementation (Fig. 9.1).

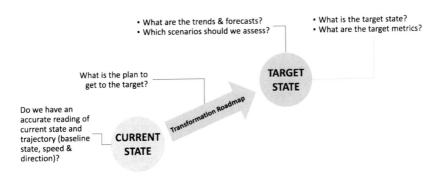

Fig. 9.1 Analytics execution plan

Criticize the Plan

Once a plan has been established, engage the stakeholders in an open discussion to criticize and review the plan. These discussions will serve to identify decisions and processes that may need to be modified or factored into the analytics model.

At times, such discussions may necessitate the reframing of the decision need, and that is quite acceptable. Once possible challenges are identified and factored in, there is less reluctance from the stakeholders to accept the decision model (Fig. 9.2).

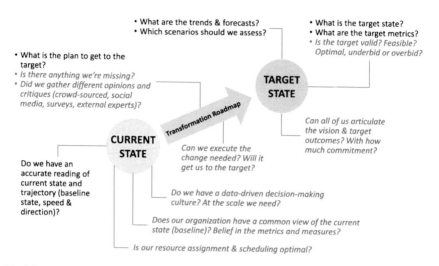

Fig. 9.2   Analytics execution plan - enhanced

The questions in this stage address three aspects:

1.   Feasibility optimality, risks, and chances of success
2.   Understanding and buy-in (commitment) from stakeholders
3.   Analytics maturity—the maturity-level determines the decision-making culture, belief in the metrics, and ability to set and navigate the path to improvement.

Execute the Plan, Re-assess at Checkpoints

Ensure that the plan has checkpoints built into allow for assessment of progress. This is especially critical when long execution time lines are involved. A review of the plan should be called with the stakeholders at each of these checkpoints to apprise them of progress. These checkpoints also allow for the necessary learning loop that enables appropriate course correction in the decision frame or model should unforeseen challenges come up during execution (Fig. 9.3).

The questions in this stage help you learn and adjust.

1.   Learn from the past:
    a.   Was the baseline accurate?
    b.   How well did we drive value realization?
    c.   Did our organization align to the change?
    d.   Did we get where we planned to be?

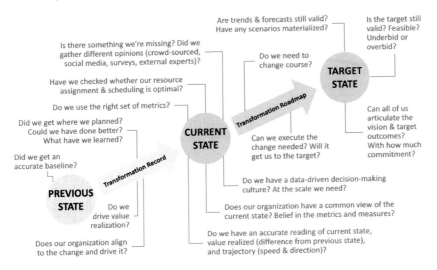

Fig. 9.3 Analytics plan execution checkpoints

    e.   Could we have done better?

    f.   What did we learn from the journey so far?

2. Review the present

    a.   Do we have the right set of metrics? Can we accurately measure our goals, current state, trajectory, and value realized?

    b.   Is our plan optimal? Have we assigned resources optimally?

    c.   Have we tested our odds of success (learn by asking, by experiment, or by expertise)

    d.   Do we have the data-driven decision making culture at the scale and maturity we need?

    e.   Do we have an analytics capability at the scale and maturity we need to provide believable and accurate navigation from idea to execution?

3. Re-assess the target

    a.   Is the target still valid and feasible? Are we still committed to it? Should we adjust it?

    b.   What is the status of the trends that we had planned to ride? Have any of the scenarios in our scenario-analysis materialized?

    c.   Will the current plan bridge the gap to the target state? Can we execute the plan? Do we need to change the plan?

Circumstances always change, but a resilient "value management" method provides the smartest course of action for the organization. This is how you make an organization smarter. As the questions in the method reveal, it takes guts and maturity to take this path—so organizational smartness requires the analytics "culture" maturity that we introduced earlier in this chapter.

Chapter 10
Building the Analytics Capability

In this chapter, we address how to structure and manage the analytics capability. To do this, managers set up teams and establish the processes, skills, and systems they need to enable sets of people to work together effectively and efficiently.

Analytics Ecosystem

The analytics function cannot be the locus of all the analytics assets (and talent) for the organization—it is, instead, a capability that enables the effective use of analytics. To do so, it integrates with its business and IT counterparts and connects with analytics providers to create an ecosystem or an analytics supply chain that has the capabilities required to address the various opportunities and the governance, processes, skills, and systems needed to do so systematically and reliably (Fig. 10.1).

We have discussed the roles of Business and IT for analytics earlier. The Analytics Providers introduced above are the organizations that provide various elements of analytics capabilities:

1   Education and Research Institutions such as university departments provide the trained people needed to work for analytics. They also increase the knowledgebase of analytics by conducting research and publishing papers. They can also provide continuing education on the subject.
2   Tools providers such as IBM, SAS, etc. build commercial software for analytics. They provide an alternative for open source efforts such as COIN-OR[1] and the R Project.[2]

---

[1] http://www.coin-or.org/

[2] http://www.r-project.org/

R. Saxena and A. Srinivasan, *Business Analytics*, International Series in Operations Research & Management Science 186, DOI: 10.1007/978-1-4614-6080-0_10, © Springer Science+Business Media New York 2013

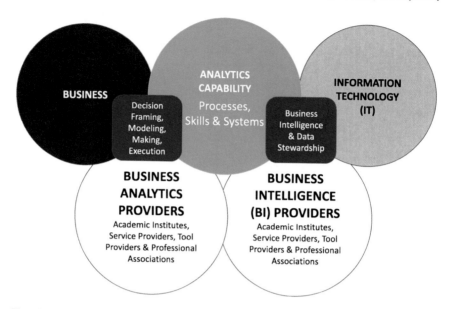

Fig. 10.1 Analytics ecosystem

3   Consulting firms and service provider organizations have skilled practitioners that can assist with any part of analytics—ranging from building specialized models to enabling an analytics-driven business transformation.

4   Professional Associations or Guilds such as INFORMS[3] or the American Statistical Association[4] provide professional affiliation, foster awareness of the domain, and provide a platform for practitioners from industry and academia to interact and collaborate with each other and with tools and services providers. They can help companies benchmark and learn from each other.

   In this analytics provider ecosystem it is important to figure out the specific partnering strategy for the organization. Analytics is a core or mission-critical function, but analysts know that they cannot become experts in all the aspects of analytics. To effectively deliver an analytics capability to their business customers they need to assist with decision framing, decision making, and decision execution. These activities focus mainly on the organization's internal knowledge. Decision modeling, on the other hand, requires analysts to leverage the best or most appropriate techniques. This quest is best conducted not in the domain of all analytics capabilities as represented by the ecosystem, not limited to just the techniques the organization's in-house analysts know. The decision modeling activity can inherently amenable to fan out to the best providers and be coordinated by the in-house capability. The other internal-facing capabilities also benefit from the provider ecosystem—they draw tools, talent, services and method from it.

The interface with IT includes the Business Intelligence (BI) and Data Stewardship functions. BI providers constitute their own ecosystem that assists with the BI and Data Stewardship tools, talent, services and methods. The BI provider ecosystem overlaps with the Business Analytics ecosystem but remains distinct—for example the key BI conferences, professional associations and service providers, such as TDWI[5] and Gartner,[6] are rooted in the IT industry.

Placing Analytics Capabilities in the Organization

What are analytics capabilities, and how do we position the analytics capability in the context of Business & IT? As with any business function, opinions differ as to whether to centralize it, distribute it to strategic business units, make a hybrid such as a mesh or hub-and-spoke model, etc.

These are the factors to consider in locating the analytics capability:

- The factors that centralize analytics into an analytics hub are related to getting economies of scale and scope from analytics talent, tools, systems, and processes
- Alignment to business units is driven by the need to improve the interlock for decision support—i.e., for analysts to work more closely with business counterparts on modeling, making, and executing decisions
- In the rare cases where analytics is aligned to IT, it is to gain benefits from leveraging the BI infrastructure more effectively
- Outsourcing the analytics capability can reduce the risk of building the analytics capability in-house, and also enable access to the service provider's economies of scale and scope.

As a consequence of analytics being viewed as mission-critical it is nearly impossible to entirely centralize analytics teams. Business units and IT organizations almost always retain a part of the analytics capabilities and we end up with analytics teams and functions distributed in different organizations and locations. In many cases these analytics nodes get linked together informally or formally into one of the distributed organizational models like matrix-management, peer-to-peer mesh with councils and governance to drive interlocks, or hub-and-spoke models that are variants on matrix reporting models (the spoke nodes may solid-line report to the analytics hub and dotted-line to their business customers or vice versa, and the hub may coordinate with business units directly in governance forums).

---

[5] http://tdwi.org/

[6] http://www.gartner.com/

In our view the most common bottleneck for analytics today is the business' ability to demand and use it. It is rare to find cases where the business organization is highly mature about its use of analytics and has milked its benefits to the point where the economies accruing from centralizing analytics are better than the benefits of effective usage that come from keeping analysts closely intertwined with the business.

In the same vein, the value of bringing in analytics support from external providers is often supported by cost/benefit analyses that trade off against delays to support each request in-house. A series of such analyses should, instead, be modeled as a demand pipeline and the analytics supply chain should be designed to be responsive (in terms of cycle times), effective in terms of delivering the right support and driving the best results, as well as cost-efficient. The variety of analytics needs for a business is such that it usually requires a dispersed and diverse supply chain—but the discipline of designing such a supply chain is not in wide use, and businesses often have no choice but to use their "assigned" provider of analytics.

Another viewpoint in this debate is the tension between getting two kinds of analytics capabilities:

1   Fast & focused analytics, that react quickly to business needs and provide deliverables focused on the demand
2   Standardized analytics delivered at scale to the enterprise, that drives consistency and eliminates duplication of effort and costs

Why can't we have both? We certainly can, if we design the capability correctly to contain both agile and standardized delivery processes. The answer relates to the workflow model used for analytics, and has nothing to do with where the analytics capability reports into. We will have more on this design later in the chapter.

Analytics Team Skills and Capacity

The six functions of analytics have been identified earlier. To specify and size the capacity we need to assess the business demand. In this situation, the commitment of business stakeholders to use analytics plays the primary role—it is best to design the supply to match the demand. The demand is often aligned to the stakeholder departments—Marketing, Sales, e-commerce, Finance, Manufacturing, Supply Chain, Services, Strategy & Planning, Human Resources, etc. Analyze the demand to place it in the context of the six functions of analytics. At this point you are in the Decision Framing function.

- Some people ask for reports and dashboards to help drive an existing initiative. Assess how much help they need in modeling (designing the right metrics and the most effective presentation), data stewardship, BI, and execution.
- When the demand is for help with designing a sales incentive program, analyze what kind of help is needed—it can range from simple spreadsheet-based

scenario analysis to a sophisticated model that uses fine-grained sales forecasting to drive assignment of sales territories and setting individual incentive targets (Fig. 10.2).

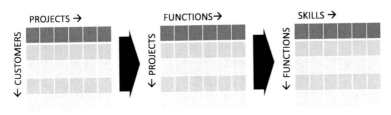

Fig. 10.2 Analytics skills requirements

Develop a model of the skill-capacities needed based on the demand. This requires us to move from the customer/project view (used to make a master list of projects that may cut across stakeholder functions) to the project/function view and then to the function/skills view. A simple diagram for this process is depicted here. The real analysis includes the timeframes and the projects become "workload forecasts" that contain a mix of new projects and sustaining/operational commitments.

The need to model the skills capacity takes us into the question of assigning people with these required skills into roles that are coherent from a talent management perspective—skills need to be bundled into roles that constitute a job description and jobs can be arranged in a matrix that allows for upward and lateral moves. We suggest developing a small set of roles for the analytics team, and tag skills to the roles to avoid a proliferation of skills making the model intractable. This becomes the job-role strategy or "competency model" for the analytics organization.

The diagram below depicts how a set of nine roles (or competencies) align to the six functions of analytics (Fig. 10.3).

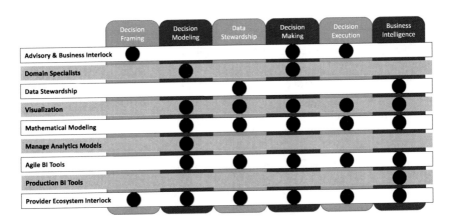

Fig. 10.3 Analytics roles and functions

Each role contains job descriptions that include skills requirements and proficiency levels, as well as tie into career paths.

- Advisory & Business Interlock roles demand customer-facing skills, business understanding, as well as an understanding of analytics. The role often includes helping with decision execution and decision making in an "Analyst" capacity, and can include playing the "Advisor" role in the decision making function. This role is usually required to drive the analytics culture and is usually asked to measure and drive the value of analytics.
- Domain specialists focus on one area such as digital marketing, Six Sigma, customer surveying, factory scheduling, financial planning, etc.—as opposed to the cross-domain "horizontal" role played by Advisory. They are brought into projects as specialists.
- Data stewardship roles perform the key function of managing the data used for analytics. They have a deep understanding of the data stewardship processes, methods, and tools; and also must develop an intimate understanding of the datasets they manage. The role includes interfacing with their BI counterparts and also to work closely with modelers to understand and supply data needs.
- Visualization roles build data visualizations appropriate to the model. They are proficient with designing data visualizations, reports, dashboards, and presentations. Since this role serves a broad set of customers, they have an understanding of the overall business and analytics domains.
- Mathematical modeling roles develop models using techniques such as linear programming, simulation, regression analysis, etc. These roles are staffed by people who have strong mathematics skills and who have an interest in applying these skills for business benefit.
- Managing analytics models is required to ensure the health and correct usage of the various analytics models in use ... including the model used to run the analytics capability. Models need to be managed as any other IP asset, and also as part of the working "machinery" of the organization.
- Agile BI Tools roles are needed to rapidly build analytics tools in response to business needs. This role is needed to provide agility for the analytics team, and is staffed with people who understand how to build analytics tools quickly.
- Production BI Tools are required to provide reliable and ongoing operation of BI tools. This role should be a hand-off from the Agile BI Tools role, so as to seamlessly enable the move from rapid experimentation to ongoing delivery of analytics tools. This role understands how to create and operate reliable, maintainable and scalable tools.
- Provider ecosystem interlock enables the relationships with providers that the analytics capability can draw upon to execute its workloads and to chart its path towards greater business relevance and maturity. This role helps the organization make informed decisions about partnering, and also helps benchmark other teams, bring in best practices from the ecosystem, and provide visibility to industry trends.

There are two common skills needed for all roles:

- Project Management and exposure to the foundational principles of managing people, politics, products and processes.
- Communication skills, methods and technologies that enable effective collaboration throughout the project cycle, from effective information-gathering to collaborative decision support and change management.

Analytics Scheduling and Workflow

To bootstrap, run, and evolve the analytics capability, the workflow has to be designed to rapidly and effectively work with business stakeholders to address their projects—take their needs from idea to execution. Do this with a "rapidly prototype" method that seeks for and locates valuable analytics. Where there is ongoing need for the same idea-to-execution process and models to be reused and scaled, invest in BI tools and ongoing process support. The agile and production analytics threads form two main branches in the workflow depicted in the diagram below, and are constantly tested to generate business value (Fig. 10.4).

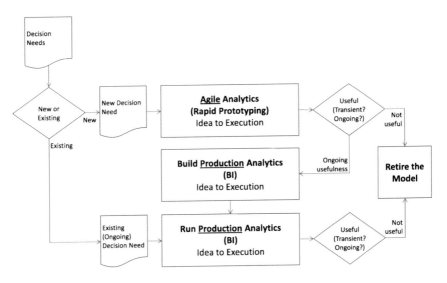

Fig. 10.4 Agile and production analytics

Scheduling this workflow is constrained by the skills and capacities in the team. Where there is a shortage of capacity, and there often is, we often find a "governance" process inserted upstream of delivery (whether agile or production). This process can be informed by the value analysis of the decision need and potentially become part of a scheduling algorithm ... but in most cases we find analytics teams workload scheduling remains as fraught with political (non-transparent) scheduling as other schedule-optimization problems in the organization. We hope to see this change, as the science of analytics wins more ground against irrationality, especially in its core application as a method to allocate scare resources.

As the analytics capability grows and ages, it generates a collection of Idea-to-Execution analytics models, each model serving a particular type of decision need. Over time, some needs lose value. At this time we must decide to retire analytics models when they are no longer useful—they are often kept in archive so that the embodied knowledge is not lost.

Tracking the Value of Analytics

There is a need to track the value of analytics so that we can schedule, size, and plan the analytics capability effectively. This simple need requires that each Idea-to-Execution analytics model be tested for value generated. Value is assessed by assessing costs, benefits (tangible and intangible), and risks.

It turns out to be very useful to periodically publish the value of analytics to various stakeholders so that they can be reminded of the value of the analytics capability. Such communication also helps create a spirit of competitive benchmarking for the use of analytics—not just within a company but in the industry. To foster the race to value, professional institutes such as INFORMS offer annual prizes to the teams that demonstrate the best uses of analytics.

Analytics Maturity Model

Analytics teams can not only measure themselves by the value they generate, they can also navigate a path towards increasing the use of analytics in their organization.

To do this, we propose the use of an "Analytics Maturity Model". The model has three dimensions: capability, culture, and technology. The culture and technology factors were discussed in earlier chapters. Here we add the analytics *capability* dimension to provide the full view of the analytics maturity model.

1   **Capability**: does the analytics team leverage the spectrum of analytics techniques

  i   Get data, measure and improve data quality
  ii   Observe, understand and explain business issues—create analyses, generate insights, monitor execution, and guide value realization
  iii Forecast trends, predict outcomes and behaviors (assess possibilities)
  iv   Formulate, simulate, and assess scenarios, develop ideas and courses of action (develop ideas)
  v   Recommend courses of action (select the best ideas: feasible and optimal or Pareto optimal)

2   **Culture**: how readily do business people use the analytics?

i   Unaware of how analytics can help
ii   Aware of analytics but do not use it for various reasons (not available, poor quality, cannot trust or understand the analytics, etc.)
iii Use analytics when it is available
iv   Support the creation and usage of analytics
v   Leader in using analytics, recognize applicability, and demand the best analytics

3   **Technology**: do the analytics teams get the systems, tools and infrastructure support they need?

i   Unable to provide analytics systems (data, tools and infrastructure)
ii   Partially provides the analytics systems and data required and refreshes the data periodically for off-line analyses
iii Fully provides analytics systems and refreshes the data periodically for off-line analyses
iv   Enables analytics to be executed in-line, i.e., used seamlessly within business processes
v   Delivers enterprise-wide in-line analytics, so the organization can use analytics at scale and without delay.

We can map organizations in a three-dimensional matrix, a cube with 125 cells, but we think that the bulk of organizations live in a small set of cells. We often see overshoot in the cells for Capability and undershoot (or lag) in Technology—analytics teams are generally eager to do more, and BI teams are generally understaffed and underfunded.

We believe that navigating the journey to improve analytics is assisted by keeping the culture, capability, and technology aspects aligned and evolving in tandem.

Chapter 11
Analytics Methods

Analytics comes from people—someone (or some team) conceives an idea, frames it, makes a model, gets the data needed to make it work, fiddles with the model until the results look useful, uses it to make decisions gets the decisions, drives implementation, and measures the results. Analytics provides fertile soil for ideas, and decision models are ideas—sometimes hugely influential ideas. The model has to be relevant (define and solve a decision need) as well as scientific (able to produce an answer or a set of answers that can be tested). We assert that unless the decision making method addresses all six analytics functions, it will not yield optimal results.

There are different methods for making and using analytics in different contexts. Here are four examples that tie all six functions in the analytics domain:

1. Process Value Management (Experiment to Evolve).
2. Capability Value Management.
3. Organizational Value Management.
4. Concept to Value Realization.

Each of these methods requires planning and execution of the analytics workload that we'll address in the chapter on Decision-analytics Teams and Systems.

Process Value Management (Experiment to Evolve)

The experimentation method is used to continuously evolve key processes used by the organization. The approach is most applicable to processes that have embedded decision making events (Fig. 11.1).

R. Saxena and A. Srinivasan, *Business Analytics*, International Series in Operations Research & Management Science 186, DOI: 10.1007/978-1-4614-6080-0_11, © Springer Science+Business Media New York 2013

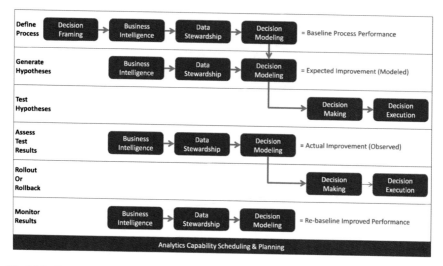

Fig. 11.1 Process value management

1. **Define the Process**: This step is used develop a clear understanding of the process we are trying to evolve. This step requires the creation of the process' decision model and baseline performance.

2. **Generate Hypotheses**: Create a hypothesis that a different workflow can lead to better results (e.g., serving up a different web-page will increase the propensity to buy or a different sales campaign will yield better results). We represent this as a "data collection" step, as hypotheses need to be introduced and assessed so that their value can be forecast.

3. **Test the Hypotheses**: This moves the new workflow into limited execution where we test hypotheses as a set of experiments where results can be tested against those from a control groups.

4. **Assess Test Results**: Check if the experiment works better than the control group, assess the underlying reasons—we want to confirm that the change we introduced caused the improved results.

5. **Rollout or Rollback**: If the experiment works better than the control group, roll out the new workflow to the applicable domain (e.g., to all car insurance buyers whose policies will lapse tomorrow). This moves the new workflow into full execution. If not, roll back the experiment (stop it).

6. **Monitor Results**: This step is used to check whether the expected improvement occurs. Track the win and the learning.

The process cycles through the analytics functions multiple times, and in world-class analytics teams this happens fast. Thus the speed (cycle time) of each cycle of process evolution is so fast that the organization can strategically outrun its competitors due to the improved performance of its core process. This is an example of how analytics converts core process from a commodity to be characterized by performance, benchmarked and "arrived at" into a strategic differentiator characterized by the rate of improvement of the process performance.

Capability Value Management

Organizations use analytics to monitor, control, and evolve capabilities such as "listen to customers" (using survey feedback methods, behavioral analyses, wallet-share analyses, etc.) or "deliver systems integration projects" (using a set of people, methods, and tools to win and execute projects).

1. **Define the Capability**: This step is used develop a clear understanding of the capability that we are focused on. Since capability modeling is an immature domain, it is sufficient for us to create a "decision frame" that defines the capability and its objectives.
2. **Design the Control System**: In this step we define the decision model that we'll use to monitor and manage the capability. This includes defining the metrics, dashboards, reports and alerts we'll use.
3. **Set up Data Stewardship**: Once the model is accepted, we need to set up a data stewardship mechanism to ensure access to "trusted data" of sufficient quality to drive the model. This includes the work needed for ongoing data assessment, cleansing, validation, enrichment, andmaintenance of data dictionaries (metadata).
4. **Monitor the Capability**: The control system generates decision-making inputs using trusted data flows. Decisions need to be taken on an ongoing basis as defined in the control system, and moved into execution. Ongoing monitoring provides the closed-loop sense and respond processes needed for the organization to execute as planned.
4. **Evolve the Control System**: On schedule or on demand, we can fork off a branch of the control system to see if we can evolve it to perform better. This evolution ripples back to the data stewardship mechanism to also evolve to meet the proposed control system dema nds. Then we assess the new control system to ensure it is an improvement over the current system. This may require a parallel-testing run or limited (pilot) deployment of the new model. If the results are good, we can go to the next step of deploying the new control system to evolve the capability.
5. **Evolve the Capability**: With every improvement of its control system, the performance of the capability also evolves. Evolution can be "functional" (e.g., increased throughput or quality) or "foundational" (e.g., increased reliability or improved back-up). Ongoing evolution is needed for the organization to continuously improve its capability to execute (Fig. 11.2).

Organizational Value Management

This method is used to define what the organization plans to become, to make the roadmap for realizing the plan, and to govern the organization's journey (Fig. 11.3).

1. **Define the Current State**: In this data-gathering step, we define the "current state" as a set of capabilities and as a baseline for performance. We also list out problems and opportunities. To do this, we start with framing the decision using both external and internal profile diagrams (context and capabilities).

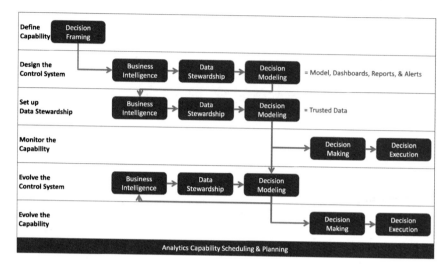

Fig. 11.2 Capability value management

Next come data collection and assessment activities. From this decision frame and data we build a model for the current state and use it to establish baseline metrics such as market share, order-to-cash cycle-time, inventory turns, etc.

2. **Define the Vision State**: In this step, we define what the organization wants to become. This "vision state" reflects the goals and aspirations of the organization, and is used to orient everybody to the common cause of getting there. The vision state is generally a lot better than the current state in key aspects, and stakeholders agree to make it their objective to get there. Determining the vision state requires revisiting the decision frame, data gathering, assessment, and modeling

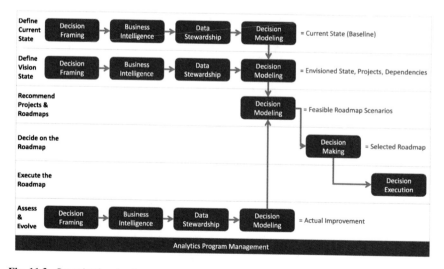

Fig. 11.3 Organizational value management

to identify trends, forecasts, aspirations, etc. Vision is set in group decision-making settings that are used to establish the "vision state" decision frame and the new decision model. The decision model for the vision state includes strategic scorecards (metrics portfolios for quantitative views) as well as scenarios, journey maps, and milestones for qualitative planning and tracking.

3. **Recommend Projects and Roadmaps**: In this decision modeling step, we build recommendations on how to close the gap between the current and vision states. These are in the form of a set of initiatives, programs, or projects that interlock to cover the gaps. An initiative in this context may contain several internal analytical requirements, e.g., an initiative to improve customer service can include within it the requirement for optimizing rosters of call center agents or optimizing maintenance inventory. The deliverable is a set of projects and a set of feasible roadmaps that satisfy project dependencies. These are often arranged into logical groupings (phases, programs, etc.). The recommendations also include the governance mechanism to guide and drive the required transformation.

4. **Decide on the Roadmap**: In this decision making step, the recommendations are reviewed, modified if needed, and a roadmap is selected.

5. **Execute the Roadmap**: After the roadmap decisions get made, they are to be acted upon. This step makes the decision translate to action and results. Funds must get allocated, leaders nominated, teams formed. Governance and tracking meetings are established to issue directives and ensure execution. In many cases you need to communicate, convince, and sustain commitment to the required actions. You may also need to recognize and reward people who act as desired, and to penalize undesirable behaviors.

6. **Assess and Evolve**: In this crucial last step, you assess the progress versus the vision, and the validity of the vision. If the expected results do not materialize, figure out the root cause and to improve the vision, roadmap, and execution as needed. This step can be done on a scheduled basis. Change requests to the roadmap originate here, and feed back into the Recommendations step to establish an evolutionary loop: Assess → Recommend → Decide → Execute.

Concept to Value Realization

These projects are one-shot mechanisms to go from concept to the realization of value (Fig. 11.4).

1. **Define the Problem**: This step is used develop a clear understanding of the business needs that we are asked to address, generally by a decision-maker, our client. Detailed analysis will come later—at this step it is sufficient for us to create a "decision frame" that frames a shared understanding of the needs, the project scope, our proposed approach and objectives.

2. **Build the Model**: In this step we build a first-pass decision model that we'll use to confirm our understanding of the business needs and to guide the downstream data gathering and modeling.

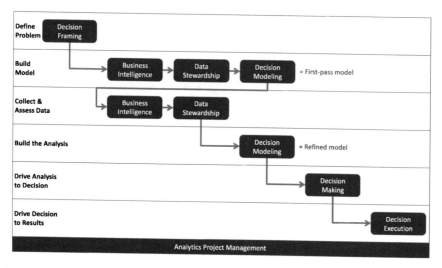

Fig. 11.4 Concept to value realization

3. **Collect and Assess Data**: Once the first-pass model is accepted, collect the data required to drive the model.
4. **Build the Analysis**: Use the data to drive the model, and use test/review cycles to refine and evolve the model until it is of sufficient quality to meet the business needs.
5. **Drive Analysis to Decision**: Present the analysis to the client and provide advisory services to drive to the decisions needed.
6. **Drive Decision to Results**: Work with the client to drive the actions needed to convert the decision to results. Track and report the outcomes and the value realized.

In many cases we find that these projects get truncated at the exit of the Analysis stage. The client gets the analysis and recommendations and may not involve the analysts in driving to the decision or to the results. In such cases the analysts lose the closed-loop learning of driving from concept to value. Worse, in the absence of the analysts the organization may not be able to use the analysis effectively—and potential value can go unrealized.

Criteria for Selecting the Analytics Method

We know that decision needs come in many different sizes and layers, so we need a stock of different analytics methods, and we often make new ones as needed. We can use rational decision-making to figure out which analytics method to use for which need.

Here is a laundry list of criteria that can be used to select the analytics method:

1. Outputs

    a. Conversion of the advice to the decision.
    b. Conversion of the decision to actions.
    c. Conversion of actions to results.
    d. Quality of the decision.

        i. Degree of confidence in its optimality. Did we frame the need correctly? Did we arrive at the best decision? How did we check that it is the best decision? When and how will we know the effects of the decision? How can we correct course if needed? Did we consider all the criteria and address/weigh them effectively? Did we consider all the feasible options?
        ii. Degree of buy-in or support by the decision-makers and stakeholders. The level of support often depends upon how inclusive and fair the decision making process is felt to be and on the acceptance of the decision-making methods. We must take care to drive out biases in the decision making process and to explain it to the participants.

2. Analytics process

    a. Speed from need-to-advice and advice-to-decision.
    b. Cost for getting from need-to-decision, which includes the cost of the resources and time taken to make the analysis and decision as well as the second-order effects of disruption or drift caused by the decision-making process.
    c. Methods: Different decision-making needs require the use of different decision-making methods, tools and techniques. Have we used the right method to make the decision?

3. Inputs

    a. Participants: Were the right people included in the process? Did they participate effectively?
    b. Data: Did we base the decision on data? Is the data of sufficient quality to support the analysis? Did we call out and test assumptions?

4. Analytics capability

    a. Analytics talent: Do we have access to talent in the organization to conduct the analyses, provide the right advice, and make the right decisions?
    b. Analytics tools: Do we have access to analytics tools, such as data-analysis software and hardware? Do we have the IT support needed to keep the technology running smoothly and reliably?
    c. Analytics processes: Do we have a set of analytics processes and techniques that we can match to the decision making needs?

Chapter 12
Analytics Case Studies

Having established a framework for analytics, we will look through a few cases of this framework in action. We present here a series of cases that each represents a "successful" application of analytics. All cases pertain to a fictitious XYZ Inc. that uses analytics heavily and successfully.

These cases are drawn from various analytical modules that the authors have been involved in developing over their professional careers (over multiple organizations) and represent a diverse sampling of various Analytical domains that the practitioner may encounter. It is important to understand that the solution recommended for each case is just one possible solution that was selected based on a variety of considerations including organizational analytical maturity, solution delivery (IT) capabilities, and speed of delivering necessary solution. The reader is encouraged to evaluate alternate solutions to each case even as an academic exercise. It is our hope that the sampling of cases presented here provide a sufficient coverage of problems and solutions in the analytics domain for the reader to appreciate the underlying similarity of structure.

We try to breakdown each case along the proposed framework and show how the framework guides one to the logical conclusion of the Analytical models.

We also assert that failure of analytical models can be traced back to an incomplete framework function, and care and diligence in establishing the framework will assist in successful deployment and use of analytics.

Before we delve into building analytical models, it is critical to understand the interplay between the proposed analytical framework and the decision layers outlined in the "Analytics Domain". Specifically, we need to understand the concept of Objective, Decision Variables, Constraints, and Parameters, of each analytical decision model.

Objective: This is the goal that we are trying to achieve with the decision that. The Objective is the focus of the "Decision Framing" exercise, and clearly calls out the criteria on which various decision options are evaluated.

Decision Variables: These are variable under the direct control of the decision maker. The decision maker can control the values that these variables can take independent of each other.

R. Saxena and A. Srinivasan, *Business Analytics*, International Series in Operations Research & Management Science 186, DOI: 10.1007/978-1-4614-6080-0_12,

Constraints: These are business and real world "rules" within which he decision maker has to operate. These will control the range of values that the decision variables can take.

Parameters: These are variables that can influence the outcome of the decision or the objective, but outside of the purview of the decision maker. These are built into decision models to enable "what-if" scenario evaluation capabilities in the decision models. Examples of such parameters would be Macro-Economic growth factors that can influence consumer demand. While the decision maker cannot control these factors, it is very useful for them to have these parameters in a model to evaluate scenarios for different values of the parameters.

Situational Clarifications and Assumptions: These are established by the Analyst based on discussions with the business unit (the marketing department) and play a critical role in framing the decision and in the choice of model used.

Case Study: Product Lifecycle and Replacement

XYZ operates a service and refurbishment facility that accepts products that are returned by the customer for a variety of reasons, and refurbishes or services them to be sold on the market again. Products are returned for a variety of reasons

- Returned within the 30 days of purchase as per XYZ return policy
- Returned as defective within the warranty period
- Returned at the end of a lease program (Customer had originally opted to lease the product as opposed to buy it outright).

XYZ's refurbishment facility would refurbish the returned product to meet the necessary standards to enable the product to be resold in the market as a "Certified Refurbished" product. Since the products sold by XYZ evolve rapidly and the specifications and configurations change every few months, the range of products coming in for refurbishing is extensive covering several product life cycles, including some EOL products.

The problem facing the refurbishment facility is to forecast the demand for various spares to handle the necessary service and refurbishments.

Decision Framing

Is it possible to forecast the demand for various components that will be needed to refurbish returned products, given that the products change frequently (3–6 months) and that the components that make up these new and improved products may not be compatible with older products?

Data Collection

The starting point for this analysis it to collect data about product returns. This is usually available in a product returns tracking system that keeps track of products that are returned and captures the customers reason for returning the product. This data is usually enhanced by identifying the defect (if any) and tagging the defective part to the returned product.

For every product sold, we would collect the following information

- Product code
- Sale date
- Return date
- Return reason
- Defective component SKU number

In addition to this, we would also collect data about the components that go to make up specific products, also called a **Bill of Materials**. The Bill of Materials is a fundamental requirement for the manufacture of any product and hence can be collected from an IT system that is designed to support the manufacture of this product.

Finally, not ALL products that are sold are returned, and the number of returned products depends, among other things, on the volume of the original product sold. Hence, we will have to collect historical data on product sales volumes.

Data Assessment

The assessment of collected data is straightforward in this scenario. We need to ensure that.

ALL returned products are captured in the data along with the necessary return reasons, and the defective component (if any) that maps to the Bill of Materials (BOM).

Each product code in the returns data needs to have a complete BOM to identify the components that make up the product.

We need to have a complete history of product sales for each product code. How much of a history is required will be established as we go through the Decision Modeling step.

Decision Modeling

Our first step in building this forecasting model is establishing a "Return-Rate curve" for each product. Product returns would be high within the first 30 days of purchase, since people could be returning products under the 30 day return policy in effect. Thereafter, returns are only in the case of defective parts covered by warranty. Since XYZ prides itself on providing a quality product to the customer and has a very strong QC program in place, the rate of returns for defective products/components is expected to be relatively low. We would expect to see a slightly higher returns rate at the end of 1 and 2 years from product sale, reflecting the returns of leased products. Since leasing represents a relatively small fraction of product shipments, we expect these returns to be relatively low as well.

Our first step in building this Decision Model is to establish this Return Rate curve and validate that it is stable across time for each product.

A sample Return Rate curve is reproduced below (Fig. 12.1).

Fig. 12.1 Case study–return rate curve

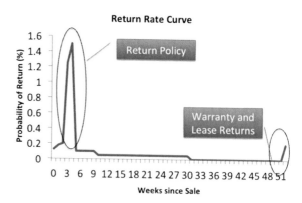

This Return Rate curve can also be interpreted as a curve of the probability of a product being returned "t" periods after product sale. We can now convert this to a "Return Volume Curve" scaling this curve by the sales volume data. Hence:

$$D_t = p_t \times S_0$$

where

S_0 is the sales volume of product at time 0

p_t is the probability of return of said system after t periods (from the Return Rate Curve)

D_t is the volume of returns of product sold in period 0 after t periods

Of course, the expected volume coming in on a particular day is an aggregation across products sold across history. Hence:

$$V_m = \sum_{x=0}^{m} S_x \times p_{m-x}$$

where

V_m is the expected volume of returns for period m

S_x is the sales volume of the product in period x

P_{m-x} is the probability of returns of a product sold in period x after m-x periods (Current period)

Defect Attach Rate: For each return, we also identify the probability of defect on each component that makes up the product BOM. We observe that the defect rate of the various components is relatively stable and steady over time and hence we leverage this fact to assert that

$$V_{m,c} = \sum_{x=0}^{m} S_x \times p_{m-x} \times F_c$$

where

$V_{m,c}$ is the expected volume of returns for period m with component c defective

S_x is the sales volume of the product in period x

p_{m-x} is the probability of returns of a product sold in period x after m-x periods (Current period)

F_c is the defect rate of component c

Decision Making

Armed with the results of our decision model (Forecasted demand for various components over time) we can then decide the inventory policy of how many units of each component to stock at various points in time. Interestingly enough, that decision in itself can be an analytic process in itself, with the forecast output from this model being data collected and the Decision model being an inventory optimization model to determine the optimal inventory levels. That would also require additional data like replenishment lead times, cost co component procurement, inventory carrying costs etc. but is beyond the scope of this case study.

Decision Execution

The Factory or Inventory manager will be provided the forecasts as a report that he can use to determine necessary inventory levels. To make this decision, additional data will have to be made available to the manager, including current stock levels of each component. This can be achieved through a report that is refreshed and delivered at the beginning of every week that provides the current stock levels of each component and the forecasted demand and the shortfall (if any). A Sample of such a report is shown below.

SKU	On-hand stock	Forecasted demand	Shortfall
SKU123	12	48	36
SKU234	0	23	23
SKU567	−3	38	41
SKU765	138	453	315

Case Study: Channel Partner Effectiveness

XYZ Corporation sells its Business-to-Business (B2B) products through multiple channels, which include direct sales to end customers and sales through channel partners. Channel partners are identified based on their ability to reach market segments that are not accessible through direct sales. XYZ has been very successful using the direct sales channel effectively in several markets (esp. developed markets). However, the channel partner strategy has been found to be particularly effective as XYZ enters new geographical markets where purchasing behavior differs significantly from the purchasing behavior of customers in their existing markets.

While the preferred channel for XYZ remains the direct channel (Higher margins, better ownership of the customer etc.), the channel partner strategy remains a critical portion of the sales strategy to ensure sufficient market penetration. In order to maintain partner loyalty, XYZ is careful in ensuring that customers are classified into categories and are pursued by direct sales or through channel partners, never both.

Decision Framing

Customer buying behavior is varied and customers respond differently to sales pursuit through direct and channel partners. Unfortunately there is no way of ascertaining a priori, a given customers response pattern to sales pursuit. Additionally, since no customer is pursued by multiple channels, we cannot compare efficacies of strategies.

Is it possible to ascertain up-front, a given customers propensity to respond favorably to a given choice of channel strategy. Using this, can we group or segment customers to pursue using the optimal channel?

Data Collection

Customers are typically classified into a Retain, Acquire or Develop (RAD) segment, based on the total spend of that customer on XYZ products. ALL customers progress from an Acquire to a Develop and Retain (if ever), albeit at varying speed. Classification of a customer into a RAD segment is usually done based on the sales team's understanding of the customers' spending patterns. This classification typically is based on the total $ spend of that customer with XYZ. A more "scientific" approach would be use XYZ "Share of Wallet" of customers total spend on similar products.

At the minimum, we will need to collect a customer classification table that classifies each customer into the appropriate RAD segment. Additionally, total $ spend on XYZ and the customers total spend on similar products could be necessary depending on the results of the Data Assessment and Decision Modeling exercises.

We will also need to capture innate characteristics of the account like the size of the organization, total revenues, industry classification, geographical location etc. This data is usually available as public domain data and can be purchased from appropriate agencies.

Data Assessment

The minimal data that needs to be collected as outlined above is a classification of customers into the correct RAD segment. Completeness needs to ensure that ALL customers are tagged appropriately. A simple data-stewardship loop that leverages the knowledge of account managers etc., who are intimately familiar with the customer, can be established to "fill in the necessary gaps" for accounts that are not classified.

Since we are actually interested in the time bound migration of accounts from one segment to the other, this data has to be "time stamped" in that, the same data needs to be available for various points in time. Additionally, since we are interested in migration possibilities over an extended period (A quarter, year etc.) and do not seek to predict the exact time of migration, it is sufficient to obtain snapshots of this data over similar epochs (quarter, annual etc.).

We will also need to map the accounts that we are interested in, with the right Industry data that has been procured form external sources. This is a non-trivial exercise, and care should be exercised in ensuring an accurate mapping of customers with industry data.

Decision Modeling

In order to predict the propensity for a given account to migrate status under pursuit by a particular strategy, we adopt a technique that is quite common in clinical cancer research, namely—Survival Analysis. Survival Analysis seeks to analyze and predict the "survival" probability of patients under a particular course of treatment over fixed time periods.

We draw an analogy to this approach by considering each account as a "patient" and the choice of channel for sales pursuit as a "course of treatment", with desired upward migration of RAD segment as "survival".

We select the subset of data that we feed into our model based on what we would like to predict.

For instance, if we would like to predict the probability of an "A" segment customer migrating to a "D" segment, under direct sales pursuit, we take a section of data that includes all customers in a given time period that were classified as "A" category, and were pursued by the direct sales channel. We also capture, the status of this customer in the next period. (Did they remain an "A" or migrate to a "D"?)

The independent variables are chosen from account characteristics to set up the survival regression model.

Decision Making

Customers can now be scored based on their propensity to migrate from one segment to another under pursuit by a specific channel.

The scored customers are now rank ordered and a suitable cutoff is determined (based on rank or score—the top quartile or score >0.5). Customers who meet the cutoff criteria are selected for continued pursuit by the current channel and others are targeted for pursuit by alternate channels.

In some cases, the model results permit the customers to be classified based on the customer characteristics. In such a case, a simple decision tree model can be built using customer attributes that lead to a final decision regarding the choice of channel.

Decision Execution

A decision tree is built and provided as a playbook to territory sales and account managers that can easily allow them to place a particular customer to the channel that provides the best opportunity of success. A Simple playbook approach also allows sales and account managers to make a quick decision on the appropriate placement of the customer without having to use a specialized application to "Score" each customer as the lead opens up.

When implementing a solution that utilizes the playbook approach, it is important to remember that the play book needs to be refreshed periodically as more data becomes available (based on the success/failure of placement in prior periods).

Case Study: Next Likely Purchase

The marketing function of XYZ depends heavily on direct customer marketing to promote new products and services. The marketing strategy is broadly classified into an "Acquisition" strategy that is focused on acquiring "new" customers (first time buyers) and a "Penetration" strategy that is focused on repeat purchases by existing customers.

Every quarter, marketing campaigns are laid out to market new and additional products and services to existing customers to increase the penetration levels.

The marketing department would like to introduce intelligence into the campaign strategy and use analytics to increase the ROI on marketing spend. They would like to identify the "Best" customers to target in their campaigns, with the right product or services, to maximize the return on marketing spend.

Decision Framing

The unit cost of any marketing campaign if fixed and constant i.e. there is no differential in cost of marketing Product A against Product B to Customer X or

Customer Y. This is a fairly reasonable assumption to make in the case of direct marketing, since these are usually done by means of a marketing brochure mailed (physically or electronically) to the customer, or a targeted offer upon the customers next visit to the store (physical/online).

In very specific cases, this may not necessarily hold, but we will proceed under this assumption for the purpose of this illustration.

We are interested in a "Time-Bound" purchase behavior. Since marketing campaigns are refreshed and evaluated every quarter, we are interested only in the ability to identify customers and products that are likely to be successful within the tenure of the current campaign.

Based on the assumptions and objectives, we are ready to frame the decision need. Specifically, we would like to identify the combinations of customers and products (from the existing pool) that are most likely to result in a positive action (sale) within a quarter if a marketing offer is made to that customer.

Data Collection

Based on the decision framing exercise, necessary data is easily identified and can be collected. We will need a history of all purchases by all customers. At a minimum, the data should contain the following information

- Customer ID—A unique identifier that identifies the particular customer
- Product ID—A unique identifier for the purchased product
- Transaction Date—The calendar date on which the product was purchased
- Transaction Value—The $ amount of the purchase transaction.

Additional data may be needed based on the choice of Decision model as will be illustrated below.

Data Assessment

Completeness of data: The data should be complete in that, it should reflect ALL purchases made by all customers. This can be validated by comparing the total of the transaction value against audited finance reported revenues from product sales. A mismatch here indicates that certain classes of transactions may be missed. This is typically the case when transactions (sales) are done through on-line and off-line channels. IT is quite common to see that transaction records from off-line sales may be incomplete or missing altogether.

Finer levels of granularity may be established be making similar comparisons by product, time period etc.

Additional data may be needed and collected based on the data stewardship findings.

1. Classification of transactions by sales channel (On-Line and Off-Line)
2. Classification of transaction by region (To ensure that the missing data does not introduce a geographical bias).

Data Quality: The individual fields in the collected data should have legitimate values and not blanks or default values. For instance, it is quite common to find that the Customer ID field having no value or blank. This can typically be traced back to inadequacies of established IT systems that may not have the ability to capture a customer ID in off-line transactions. For example, if a customer walks into a store and purchases a product, we may miss capturing the customer ID, since no such ID is needed for a store purchase. Customers are encouraged to present such an ID in the form of loyalty cards, but when one is not presented, we have no way of ascertaining if this was an existing customer making an off-line purchase or a new customer making a first purchase! Multiple POS (Point of Sale) solutions seek to address this problem, but still remain a recurring point of failure.

Data Enhancement: After ascertaining the extent of these problems, the data can sometimes be enhanced to ensure completeness and accuracy.

1. The data typically flows through multiple systems and databases before it makes it to the analyst. These systems perform various levels of aggregation and accumulation before passing the data on to the next system. It is quite commonly observed that data transmission between systems (typically called ETL) can lead to a loss of fidelity. Such transmission losses are easily identified and corrections can be made to reduce the error.
2. Data enhancement by merging against additional data sources. Customers who purchase off-line are encouraged to "register" their purchase on the website, thereby tying the product and transaction to the customer ID. Such data, if available, can be used to enhance the base transaction data that has been collected.
3. Customer Satisfaction survey data, if available can be used to enhance the transactional data to provide insight into customer perception of XYZ products.
4. Customer Demographics, if available can be used to further enhance the data with specific customer characteristics like geographical location (City, ZIP), age, income, marital status, size of household etc. Such data is sometimes collected along with the customer satisfaction survey data.

Decision Modeling

Leading from the result of the Decision Framing exercise, the structural choice of the model is made. We wish to predict the probability that a customer will respond favorably to a marketing offer for a specific product. A multinomial logistic regression model is used with the dependent variable as the product that the customer will buy, and the independent variables chosen from the set of available variables that pass the data collection, assessment and enhancement steps.

The enhanced historical data is prepared in a structure that is amenable to such modeling. We take a snapshot of customer transaction history and establish our dependent variables as indicator variables (categorical variables) that indicate which product has been purchased in the last observed time period. For instance, if we are interested in the probability of positive response within a three-month period, we establish our indicator variables to reflect a product purchase in the last three-months of the data.

The choice of independent variables is left to the analyst and the availability of data. For instance, if only transactional data is available, the independent variables are selected from a set of possible transactional variables.

- Total number of transactions in leading up to the purchase
- Total value of such transactions
- Length of relationship with the customer (aka Time in Books)
- List of products in customer's portfolio leading up to the purchase under study.

In addition, the data enhancement process could add additional independent variables. For instance, if customer satisfaction and demographic data is available, a range of possible independent variables is made available for the model.

It is critical to ensure that all data selected for the model is complete in the set of variables chosen for the model.

Decision Making

Once the suitable model has been built, the decision making can be enabled in two flavors.

1. Select the best product for a given customer. This approach is used when a one-on-one interaction with the customer is possible (Say, when the customer contacts XYZ for support/queries). The interaction agent could use the model to determine the best product to position for the customer and act accordingly
2. Select the best set of customers to promote a particular product. This approach is used to build a promotional campaign for a given product, to identify the best set of target customers to promote the product to.

Decision Execution

To enable execution of decisions made, it is necessary to communicate the decision to the appropriate agent to execute the decision. For instance, in the first usage case outlined above, the contact center agent who interacts with the customer needs to be provided with the "Best product to position" for the customer under consideration. In the second case, the execution agent would be the

marketing or campaign manager who would distribute the promotional campaign
to the identified set of customers.

In either case, the content (Results of the Decision model) needs to be provided
at the right point to enable the agents to execute the decision appropriately. This
could be delivered by means of a Decision Execution application that allows the
agent to quickly get the appropriate results of the decision model. An example of
a decision execution application that would be used by a contact agent to identify
the best product for a given customer is shown below (Fig. 12.2).

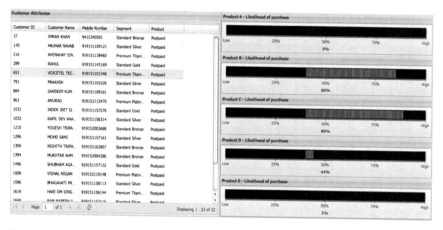

Fig. 12.2 Next likely purchase dashboard

It is important to understand that the "Carrier" of the necessary information is
not critical (It could be an IT application, a suitable Excel spreadsheet or a simple
"Play Book").

Case Study: Resource Management

Various departments in XYZ Inc. manage a large number of projects simultane-
ously to deliver services to its customers (Internal and External). These projects
are staffed with people to execute on these projects, and XYZ would like to
manage the staffing of these projects to ensure the most efficient deployment of
resources across the various projects.

Resources are located globally in various centers worldwide. XYZ uses these
global centers to leverage resources on

1. Time Zone—A "Follow the Sun" approach to task management that ensures
   work progress on any project/task 24/7 by suitably utilizing resources across
   various time zones.
2. Cost Arbitrage—Leveraging lower cost centers to optimize cost of execution.
3. Skills Arbitrage—Leveraging a Global talent pool to ensure that sufficient
   resources with appropriate skills are available.

4. Customer Local Connection—Having a Global team allows XYZ to ensure that customers worldwide have necessary support available in the region and appropriate time-zone.

Decision Framing

We would like to identify the best resources to be assigned to each task keeping the organizational and project objectives in mind. It is critical to identify the project and organizational constraints that will enable us to execute on the decisions recommended by the model.

Some examples of such constraints are:

1. A resource cannot be assigned for more than 8 h in a day.
2. A resource cannot be assigned for more than 40 h in a week.
3. A resource cannot be assigned to any task on weekends (specific to the location).
4. Resources cannot be shared across certain projects (For instance, a resource assigned to a project/task with a particular customer may be contractually prohibited from working on any project with a competitor).
5. A Project should have a minimum amount of work assigned to a resource in a particular geography.
6. Certain types of tasks have to be executed in the customers location/ geography.
7. Resource assignment should remain stable across the duration of the project to the extent possible. For instance, we should have minimal number of resource changes to execute a particular task.
8. If tasks extend beyond the scheduled date, we should be able to maintain consistency of resource assignment.

We seek to maximize the margins from the project portfolio, by choosing the best resources to assign to tasks that

1. Are qualified to perform the task
2. Meet ALL the organizational and Project constraints.

Data Collection

The Data collection for the Decision framed above is non-trivial, and can be categorized under several heads.

• Project Work Breakdown Structure—Outlines all the detailed tasks that need to be completed in order to deliver the project successfully. Successful projects require thorough planning on the part of the project manager to accomplish these tasks. The Work Breakdown Structure (WBS) serves as a guide for defining work as it relates to a specific project's objectives. The WBS includes a "Project Plan" that lays down the tasks, schedules and dependencies. In addition, the WBS includes budget and forecasts of costs and hours expected to be consumed by these tasks, and the necessary skills and competencies required for each task.[1]

- Resource Skill Inventory—This is a collection of relevant skills and competencies of each of the resources that are covered under the umbrella of the Decision Frame. For Instance, we skills, competencies and certifications of all the people we will assign to the various projects.
- Resource Calendar—This simple is the availability calendar of each project resource. People are subject to availability considerations like Time Off, Vacation, Training, etc. Visibility into the availability of resources for at any given time is essential.
- Resource Cost and Location—For every resource under consideration, we would need to know the cost and the geographical location of the resource.
- Project and Organizational constraints—These represent operational and/or contractual requirements and targets that need to be considered in building the decision model. More details and examples are provided in the sections to follow.

Data Assessment

The single most critical data element is the WBS outlined above. While the need for an accurate WBS of project success is acknowledged, accepted and documented, in practice, WBS are notoriously incomplete for various reasons, operational, system related and political. It is not unusual to have to establish a data governance loop to collect and enhance the WBS to the necessary level of detail. In some cases, a Project Management Office (PMO) is established to lay down and enforce the "rules of engagement" for Project Manages to establish a WBS of sufficient accuracy. At a minimum, the following information needs to be collected for each task that makes up the WBS.

- Task Scheduled—Start and End Date of each task
- Task Forecasted hours—The total forecasted hours necessary to complete the task
- Task skills and competency requirements
- Task location considerations (if any).

In addition, the following information could also be collected to support additional capabilities in the decision model as necessary.

---

[1] More information about Project Work Breakdown Structures can be obtained from the Project Management Institute www.pmi.org.

- Task Budgets—Budgeted hours and cost for each task.
- Task Dependencies—Predecessor and Successor tasks for each task.

Resource Data—Necessary data for the resources under consideration for the model are easier to obtain and most organizations have necessary data in various HR systems. Availability calendar and location information are the most easily sourced. Resource costing is also readily available from appropriate finance systems. Assessment of this data is limited to basic checks on completeness and elimination of duplicates.

Data Enhancement: The typical data availability and the possible dynamic nature of the data dictate that a data stewardship and enhancement loop is almost mandatory in this case. Each of the data elements outlined above can be verified for completeness and enhanced (validated) by requiring the owner of the information (Project Managers, Resource Manager, etc.) to complete any missing pieces of information.

Decision Modeling

The Modeling requirement in this case is very straight forward and the problem is modeled as a **Mixed Integer Linear Programming Problem,**[2] which is well understood and easily solved. The model chooses the number of hours that a given resource should be assigned to a given task on a given day, such that

1. The Total Margin (Project revenue–Resource cost) across all projects is maximized. If Project revenue is not available, we can choose to simply minimize the total cost of resource assignment.
2. The total hours assigned to a task across the duration of the task is AT LEAST equal to the task forecasted hours requirement.
3. A resource can be assigned to a particular task ONLY if the resource is qualified to perform the task (Match between resource skill inventory and task skill requirement).
4. ALL organizational constraints are satisfied.

Decision Making

The Decision model described above recommends optimal assignment of resources to tasks. When the model is set up accurately to reflect all the necessary considerations, the decision making is simply to accept or reject the recommendations. As the model use evolves in an organization, more business constraints are

---

[2] The Subject of Mixed Integer Linear Programming is a field of study in itself and details of the model are beyond the scope of this book. Several wonderful books are available that delve into details of this approach.

reflected accurately in the model (Enhanced data quality, improved process control etc.) and the need and justification to reject a recommendation reduces.

However, in practice, some considerations are not modeled or supported by sufficient data and hence, recommendations that violate these "External considerations" may be rejected. In such cases, the model is used iteratively by rejecting some recommendations, and re-optimizing the system with the remaining tasks and resources. Each successive iteration will add an additional constraint that expressly prohibits the assignment that was rejected in the previous iteration. The nature of such models is that it is easy to evaluate the additional "Cost" of rejecting an assignment and the decision maker can make an informed decision weighing the actual costs and perceived benefits of rejecting model recommendations.

Decision Execution

The complexity of the data required in this necessitates multiple levers of monitor and control in order to ensure execution of the decisions made.

Data quality monitoring and control: The primary source of WBS data for the model is the Project Managers who necessarily provide the WBS at a level of detail as necessitated by the model. Capturing this data requires the Project Management framework to capture this input coupled with a Project Manager data scorecard that highlights missing data elements that the Project Manager is required to provide.

Decision Acceptance Audit Trail: As discussed in the previous section, decisions recommended by the model may be accepted or rejected if those recommendations violate "External Considerations". It is critical to understand that each such rejection of a recommended solution comes at a cost, and the Manager who rejects a recommendation will have to provide sufficient justification of such rejection. The centralized PMO will be responsible for approving or over-ruling such rejections by comparing the justification against the model cost of deviating from the recommendation. An audit trail of such rejections will be maintained and used in a "feedback" loop to

- Educate the managers about compliance to optimal policies
- Train the managers to provide accurate input to prevent such external considerations
- Update the model to add such justifiable constraints into the model.

References

Bishop MA, Tout J (n.d.) 50 years of successful predictive modeling should be enough: lessons for philosophy of science. Philos Sci 68(Proceedings):S197–S208

Brache A, Rummler G (1990) Improving performance: how to manage the white space on the organization chart. Jossey-Bass, San Francisco

Carter MW, Price CC (2001) Operations research—a practical introduction. CRC Press, Boca Raton

Charan R (2006) Conquering a culture of indecision. Harv Bus Rev 84:108–117

Collier KW (2011) Agile analytics: a value-driven approach to business intelligence and data warehousing. Addison Wesley, Amsterdam

Davenport TH (2009) How to design smart business experiments. Harv Bus Rev 87:68–76

Davenport TH, Harris JG (2007) Competing on analytics. Harvard Business Press, Boston

Davenport TH, Harris JG (2007) Competing on analytics: the new science of winning. Harvard Business Press, Boston

Eisenhardt KM, Kahwajy JL, Bourgeois III L (1997) How teams have a good fight. Harv Bus Rev 75:75–85

Enders CK (2010) Applied missing data analysis. Guildford Press, New York

Friendly M (2005) Classification—the ubiquitous challenge, vol 1. Springer-Verlag, Berlin

Garvin DA, Roberto MA (2001) What you don't know about making decisions. Harv Bus Rev 79:108–16

Gawande A (2009) The checklist manifesto: how to get things right. Metropolitan Books, New York

Hammomd JS, Ralph KL, Raiffa H (2006) Hidden traps in decision making. Harv Bus Rev 76:47–48

Hammond JS, Keeney RL, Raiffa H (1999) Smart choices: a practical guide to making better decisions. Harvard Business School Press, Boston

Hilliard R (2010) Information driven business. Wiley, New York

Hillier FS, Lieberman GJ (1968) Introductions to operations research. McGraw-Hill, New York

Inmon B (1992) Building the data warehouse. Wiley, New York

Iyengar SS, Lepper MR (2000) When choice is demotivating: can one desire too much of a good thing? J Pers Soc Psychol 79:995–1006

Jensen MC (2003) Paying people to lie: the truth about the budgeting process. Eur Financ Manag 9:379–406

Kahneman D (2011) Thinking, fast and slow. Allen Lane, London

Kahneman D, Klein G (2009) Conditions for intuitive expertise: a failure to disagree. Am Psychol 64(6):515–526

Kahneman D, Lovallo D, Sibony O (2011) The big idea: before you make that big decision. Harv Bus Rev 89:50–60

Kimball R (1996) The data warehouse toolkit. Wiley, New York

R. Saxena and A. Srinivasan, *Business Analytics*, International Series in Operations
Research & Management Science 186, DOI: 10.1007/978-1-4614-6080-0,
© Springer Science+Business Media New York 2013

Kimball R, Caserta J (2004) The data warehouse ETL toolkit. Wiley, Indianapolis

Klein G (2007) Performing a project premortem. Harv Bus Rev 85:18–19

Michel L (2003) Moneyball. W.W.Norton and Co, New York

MIT Sloan Management Review and the IBM Institute for Business. (2010) Analytics: the new path to value. MIT Sloan Management Review and the IBM Institute for Business. MIT Sloan Management Review Research Report Fall 2010

Pfeffer J, Sutton RI (2006) Evidence-based management. Harv Bus Rev 84:62–74

Polikoff I, Coyne R, Hodgson R (2005) Capability cases: a solution envisioning approach. Addison-Wesley, Upper Saddle River

Pomerol J-C, Barba-Romero S (2000) Multicriterion decision in management. Springer, Berlin

Roy D (1952) Quota restriction and goldbricking in a machine shop. Am J Sociol 57(5):427–442

Surowiecki J (2004) The wisdom of crowds. Anchor, New York

Taha HA (2011) Operations research: an introduction. Prentice Hall, New Jersey

Tao R, Liu S, Huang C, Tam C (2011) Cost-benefit analysis of high-speed rail link between Hong Kong and Mainland China. J Eng Proj Prod Manag 1(1):36–45

Tavares LV, Weglarz J (1990) Project management and scheduling. Springer, Berlin

Tavares VL (1998) Advanced models in project management. In: Hillier F (ed) Springer, Berlin

Index

A

Action taken, 105, 116
Actionable analytics, 116
Adaptive decision needs, 14
Adoption, 49, 55, 81, 83, 91
Advisor, 18, 74, 118, 127
Agility, 87, 128
Airline partnership model, 22, 24–26
Alerting decisions, 11
Alerts, 11, 14, 16, 26, 60, 62, 81, 111, 135
Analyst, 3, 4, 18, 21, 22, 29, 37, 68, 70, 97,
    101, 109, 110, 116, 127, 142, 151
Analytical models, 90, 97, 98, 104, 141
Analytical tools, 96, 98
Analytics capability, 124, 125, 128–130
Analytics culture, 114, 115, 117, 118, 127
Analytics domain, 6, 9, 15, 34, 133, 141
Analytics ecosystem, 118, 123, 124
Analytics maturity model, 130
Analytics solution providers, 86
Analytics team, 1, 3, 126–128, 130
Anchoring, 75
Ancillary analytics, 117
Artificial neural networks, 48
Assessment, 79, 105, 110, 118, 143, 147, 149,
    155
Assignment and dispatch decisions, 11, 60
Availability, 12, 28, 75, 154, 155

B

Baseline of the current state, 54
Behavior changes, 81
Benchmarking, 45, 47, 88, 90, 130
Best practices, 51, 128
Biases, 10, 32, 34, 74, 76, 139
Big data, 35–37, 39

Big models, 35–37
Bottlenecks, 45, 60, 80, 81
Bounded rationality, 74, 75
Bubble, 37
Business analysts, 3, 17, 108
Business analytics databases, 87, 88, 94
Business analytics ready database, 95
Business intelligence, 4–6, 85–89, 125
Business policies, 110, 111
Business transformation, 47, 124
Buy-in, 18, 97, 120, 139

C

Capability layer, 12, 13, 16, 24, 43, 46
Capability models, 16, 43, 44, 56, 128
Capability reference models, 44
Capability value management, 135, 136
Case trackers, 110
Causality chains, 55
Cause-effect chains, 15
Centralized repository, 92
Channel partner effectiveness, 146
Checkpoints, 55, 56, 120, 121
Checks and balances, 18, 71
Clashing analyses, 18
Closed-loop, 10, 135, 138
Closed-loop analytics systems, 87
Collaboration, 3, 5, 33, 68, 97, 129
Complementors, 41
Complex event processing, 62
Compliance, 60, 71, 156
Concept to value realization, 137, 138
Confirmation bias, 33, 74
Context diagrams, 32–34, 42
Continuous value management, 57
Control systems layer, 12, 14, 25, 27

C (*cont.*)

Control systems modeling, 47
Control views, 57
Controlled experiments, 16, 52
Conversation, 33, 36, 82
Corrupt data, 103
Counter intuitive, 75
Cross functional flowcharts, 45
Crowdsourcing, 49, 50
Cutover, 81

D

Damping level, 70
Dashboard, 34, 57, 96, 114, 152
Data arrival stage, 87, 104
Database designs, 87, 94
Data dictionary, 107, 111, 112
Data driven, 4, 9, 13, 58, 74, 76, 119
Data driven decision culture, 67, 76, 121
Data enrichment, 106, 108
Data infrastructure, 3, 85–87
Data loading, 92, 95
Data loss, 105
Data manipulation, 93
Data mart, 94, 95, 98
Data problem, 110
Data quality issue, 93
Data repository, 92, 93
Data scrubbing, 105, 106
Data security, 104
Data sourcing, 89, 104
Data stewardship, 6, 34, 93, 96, 97, 102, 105,
    106, 125, 127, 135, 147, 155
Data transformation, 94
Data visualization, 34, 42, 47, 55, 61, 96
Data warehousing, 4, 5
Debate, 38, 68, 72, 126
Decide, 11, 22, 72, 115, 137, 145, 148, 151, 155
Decision execution, 7, 80–83, 92, 145, 148,
    151, 152, 156
Decision framing, 6, 19, 20, 22, 28, 141, 142,
    146, 148–150, 153
Decision layers, 10, 13–15, 22, 141
Decision maker, 18, 67, 68, 141, 142
Decision making, 4, 7, 10, 17, 18, 67–69, 73,
    74, 77, 127, 137, 145, 148, 151, 155
Decision making method, 69, 73, 133
Decision making roles, 18, 73
Decision model, 6, 19–21, 25, 26, 31, 63, 64,
    69, 70, 73, 119, 137, 145, 155
Decision modeler, 68
Decision modeling, 6, 32, 59, 63, 64, 67, 124
Decision need, 16, 20, 21, 24–26

Decision pathway, 71
Decision process, 69, 71, 73
Decision record, 69
Defensive analytics, 117
Degree of change, 36, 38
Deliverable (analysis), 137
Devil's advocate, 73, 77
Dispatch, 11, 60, 61

E

Early-warning system, 81
Economies of scale, 1, 125
Ecosystem, 15, 16, 36, 39–44, 63, 67, 70, 86,
    113, 118, 123–125, 128
Emotions, 74
ERP systems, 85
Events, 11, 14, 26, 58–60, 62, 69, 71, 133
Evidence-based management, 76
Exception lists, 81
Expectations, 28, 29, 102, 103
Expertise, 7, 11, 16, 18, 47–49, 53, 58, 61, 80,
    86, 107, 121
Expertise models, 16, 49
Extract-transform-load, 92

F

Fast and focused analytics, 126
First-cut review of the data, 102
First-pass yield, 42, 61
Fishbone diagrams, 45
Fitness for use, 6, 103
Flowcharts, 45, 60
Football, 48
Forecasting model, 63, 92, 143
From the gut, 37
Full spectrum of business needs, 2

G

Gold standard, 49
Groupthink, 72, 77

H

Hierarchies, 87, 90, 91, 97, 107–110
High fidelity, 87, 90, 106
High speed rail corridor, 39
Histograms, 34, 102, 103

I

Illusions, 76
Indecision, 75

Indexing, 48
Industrial engineering, 3
Influence diagrams, 55
Information technology, 3
Initial data provision, 101
Inline analytics, 26, 59, 98
Input data, 87–89, 95, 96
Integrity, 62, 93, 95, 101, 103
Intelligent assistants, 60
Internet, 39, 86, 91
Internet of things, 39
Intuition, 47, 75
Irrationality, 67, 68, 76, 77, 118, 119, 130

L

Leadership, 18, 36, 38, 116
Learning by asking, 16, 49, 51
Learning by experiment, 16, 51
Learning curves, 58
Learning loop, 21, 48, 49, 58, 70, 120
Learning-by-asking models, 16
Learning-by-experiment models, 16
Legacy systems, 86
Lies, damn lies and statistics, 118
Log-file, 95, 96
Loss aversion, 74
Low hanging fruit, 64, 111

M

Machine to machine (m2m), 39
Making decisions, 67–69, 74, 117
Management information systems, 3
Manufacturing execution systems, 11
Markov chains, 35, 48
Master data management, 106
Matching, 106
Mathematical models, 34, 35, 42, 43, 48
Maturity, 89, 114–116, 120, 121, 128, 130, 141
Megatrend, 37
Meta data management, 97
Metaphors, 33
Microsoft excel, 12, 97
Misrepresentations, 75
Mixed integer linear programming, 155
Model data, 87
Motivational context, 82, 83
Motivations, 82
Multi criteria decision models, 64

N

Natural experiments, 16, 52, 53
Network layer, 12, 13, 23–25, 36, 43, 46
Network management systems, 11

Next likely purchase, 20, 148
Normal distribution, 75, 103

O

Obsolete rules, 118
Offensive analytics, 117
Offline analytics, 26, 59, 98, 131
OLAP, 95
OLTP systems, 90, 99
On demand, 11, 71, 135
On schedule, 57, 71, 135
Ongoing data assessment, 104, 105, 135
Ongoing data provision, 104
Ongoing data sourcing, 104, 105
Ongoing data stewardship, 105
Operational data store, 93–95
Operational intelligence, 59
Operations research, 2–4, 12
Optimization systems modeling, 58
Optimization systems models, 16
Organizational intelligence, 10
Organizational value management,
    133, 135
Outcomes, 6, 11, 13, 31, 47–50,
    82, 130, 138
Overconfidence, 74
Overlapped analytics systems, 87

P

Pareto optimal, 64, 130
Parsing, 106
Perverse effects, 82
Pestle, 40
Poisson distribution, 103
Porter five forces, 41
Porter value chain, 42
Predictable domain, 47
Prediction markets, 50
Premortem, 73
Pricing model, 16, 17
Priming, 75
Privacy, 104
Proactive decision needs, 14
Process decisions, 11, 67, 133
Process execution, 11, 60
Process value management (experiment to
    evolve), 133
Processes and procedures, 80
Product lifecycle, 40, 142
Professional associations, 124, 125
Program managers, 81
Provide incentives, 81
Purpose, mastery and autonomy, 83

Q

Quality circles, 118
Quality control, 3, 62
Quality function deployment, 109
Quasi-experiment, 53

R

Rapidly prototype, 129
Rational advice, 6
Rational decision making, 3, 10, 17–19, 68,
    74, 114, 115, 138
Rational decisions, 3, 9, 10, 15, 17–19, 68, 71,
    74–77, 114, 115, 138
Reactive decision needs, 14
Real time analytics, 11, 26, 59, 98, 99
Realization, 56, 117, 118, 130, 133, 137
Real-time analytics, 11
Recommendation engine, 47
Refurbishment, 142
Regression, 35, 48, 76, 128, 147, 150
Reports, 3–5, 62, 79–81, 92, 117, 128, 135
Resource management, 45, 152, 155
Responsiveness, 70, 94
Return rate curve, 143, 144
Risk perception, 74
Roadmap for value improvement, 54
Robust, 10, 27, 58, 64, 88

S

Sales incentives, 42, 81, 126
Supervisory control and data acquisition
    (SCADA), 11
Scaling the decision culture, 102, 103
Scatter, 34
Scatter charts, 34
Scenario, 2, 7, 13, 22, 24, 31, 48, 55, 63, 64,
    72, 73, 75, 97, 121, 127, 143
Schedule layer, 12, 14
Security, 36, 62, 63, 104
Self-correcting (learning), 10
Separation of duties, 71
Service level agreements, 105
Single criteria decision models, 64
Single-pass analytics systems, 87
Solution envisioning, 44
Staging database, 93
Stakeholders, 17–19, 28, 44, 71, 72, 74, 119,
    120, 126, 129, 130, 136, 139
Standardization, 106
Standardized analytics, 126
Star schema, 94, 95
Statistics, 2–4, 118

Stored procedures, 87, 92
Strategy layer, 12, 14
Stuff, 2, 107
Super bowl, 49
Surveillance society, 104
Survey, 16, 49, 50, 87, 90, 91, 107, 135, 150
Surveying, 49, 91, 127
Swim-lane flowcharts, 45

T

Target (future) state, 54
Target state, 53, 54, 56, 119
Third normal form, 94
Traceability, 95, 105, 112
Training, 11, 60, 77, 80, 81, 111, 154
Transparency, 62, 65
Transparent, 9, 62, 73, 74

U

Unpredictable, 9, 62, 73, 74, 129
Unreliability, 58
Urgency, 36, 38, 39, 71
User error, 111

V

Validity, 25, 50, 53, 62, 63, 112, 118, 137
Value improvement, 53–55, 58
Value improvement models, 16, 54, 55, 57
Value improvement planning, 54
Value leakage, 55, 56, 117
Value management, 55, 57, 118, 121
Value of analytics, 115–117, 127, 130
Value pools, 38
Value-chain analyses, 38
Verifiable, 9, 62
Viable system model, 14
Visualization, 34, 35, 42, 55, 58, 61, 95–97,
    128

W

Weibull distribution, 103
What you see is all there is (WYSIATI), 33
What's in it for me (WIIFM), 83
Workflow layer, 11, 13, 25, 26, 28, 59, 118
Workflow modeling, 59, 60
Workflow models, 12, 16, 17, 126

Y

Y2K (Year 2000), 85, 86

Printed by Publishers' Graphics LLC
MO20121218.10.02.620